A CRITIQUE OF
REVOLUTIONARY HUMANISM:
FRANTZ FANON

A CRITIQUE OF REVOLUTIONARY HUMANISM:
FRANTZ FANON

By

Richard C. Onwuanibe, Ph.D.

Department of Philosophy
Cleveland State University
Ohio, U.S.A.

WARREN H. GREEN, INC.
St. Louis, Missouri, U.S.A.

Published by

WARREN H. GREEN, INC.
8356 Olive Blvd.
Saint Louis, Missouri, 63132 U.S.A.

Library of Congress Catalog Card Number

ISBN No. 87527-296-7

Printed in the United States of America

iv

DEDICATION

To my parents, relatives and friends, and all dedicated to bearing witness to love and truth in spite of turmoils.

In reconciliatione stat progressio humana

FRANTZ FANON
Author of THE WRETCHED OF THE EARTH
Grove Press, April 23, 1965

BIOGRAPHICAL NOTES

The name of Frantz Fanon today rings with revolution. His complex character and its unfolding in various stages of development with corresponding activities can best be understood by beginning from his background in the French colony of Martinique where he was born in Forte-de-France on July 20, 1925. His family was, in Martinique's standards, upper middle class. And although black, the members of the family were patriotic French citizens at that time.

However, the island's connection with the metropolitan France had a certain ambivalence since French rule supported the privileged position of the middle class, Black or White, and seemed to silence any smouldering desire for political change on the part of the masses and would-be political agitators. It is interesting to note how ironic the family's situation was in view of Fanon's revolutionary commitment later on. Many admirers and critics of Fanon are puzzled by his not returning home to Martinique to conduct a revolution there. How far is the *dictum* "physician heal thyself" appropriate in his case? In answer to this question, Simone de Beauvoir's comment is in order: "His origins aggravated his conflicts: Martinique was not ripe for an uprising: what one gained in Africa would serve in the Antilles: all the same one felt his awkwardness at not struggling in his native land, and even more so, at not being a native Algerian."[1] But Fanon was not provincial in outlook. While not ignoring the "awkwardness at not struggling in his native land," one must see that his revolutionary humanism has a universalist thrust which takes concrete form wherever the circumstances are ripe; for what is important is to liberate man from dehumanization and exploration wherever these occur; the conditions in Africa were more favorable for revolution than his native Antilles.

With regard to the family's origin, Frantz's father drew from mixed Indian-Martiniquean blood. He was a government official and a freemason. Fanon's mother, an illegitimate daughter of mixed parents, had Alsatian blood in her ancestry. However, the stigma of illegitimacy was not of great social consequence. Of the eight children in the family, four boys and four girls, Frantz was the darkest in colour, and this fact appeared to be a problem for him in the family in view of the Martiniquean consciousness of gradations of colour. When Frantz was born as the fourth son, it seemed that his mother viewed him with some regret because she thought that she had had enough boys. This seemingly unwelcome attitude of his mother coloured much of the little boy's relation to his mother. He was said to have been a sensitive child, and his mother's mixed feelings toward him constituted a challenge as he was growing up.[2] This is in contrast to the picture of his mother who later became proud of his achievements.[3]

Frantz attended a segregated black Lycee which had a religious atmosphere. However, he and his brother, Joby, failed to avail themselves of the opportunity of religious education. In 1944, he enlisted in the French Army, and served in Europe under General de Lattre de Tassigny against the Germans, and distinguished himself by meriting a medal for bravery. One could imagine that Fanon would have thought that the war was for Whites and not the concern of Blacks. On the contrary, to Fanon, it was not just for liberating Whites but also for Blacks, since the liberation of humanity from all kinds of oppression and exploitation constitutes a basic principle of his social philosophy; and Blacks are part of humanity, even though they have been oppressed and exploited by Whites. One can see here that Fanon's involvement in the war as a means of destroying human oppression was a practical expression of the transcendence of his universal humanism, although the road to its fullest realization could be tortuous.

Subsequently, Fanon studied medicine and psychiatry at the University of Lyon, France. His student activities included the organization of the Union of Students from Overseas France, and being the editor of *Tam-Tam (Tom-Tom)*, their mimeographed newspaper. In 1952, he successfully defended his medical dissertation. It is significant that in dedicating it to his brother, Felix, Frantz wrote on the cover the following self-revelatory remarks:

> The greatness of a man is to be found not in the acts but in his style. Existence does not resemble a steadily rising curve, but a slow, sometimes sad series of ups and downs.
>
> I have a horror of weaknesses—I understand them, but I do not like them.

I do not agree with those who think it is possible to live life at an easy pace. I don't want this. I don't think you do either . . . [4]

Fanon's residence in Saint Alban in the summer of 1952 under the able direction of Professor Francois Tosquelles was valuable experience. Tosquelles' ideas of sociotherapy stood Fanon in good stead in his work as a psychiatrist.

Fanon returned to Martinique to work in the hospital at Vauclin as a general practitioner. As an intellectual, he was sensitive to the social and intellectual climate of the time. Among the major influences on his social thinking are Aime Cesaire, Jung, Adler, Freud, Kierkegaard, Jaspers, Nietzsche, Heidegger, Merleau Ponty, Hegel, Marx, Lenin, Trotsky, and Sartre. This was the period of his greater awareness of the colonial system which he was to denounce as racist. The Blacks were alienated individuals as a consequence of discrimination by Whites.

In 1952, he published *Peau Noir, Masques Blancs (Black Skin, White Masks)*, a clinical study of alienated Black consciousness in the colonial system. It contains psychological, psychiatric, and philosophical essays; and it is the philosophical foundation of his revolutionary humanism.

His marriage with Josie Duble, a white woman from Lyon, took place in 1953. The couple were congenial. Attractive, intelligent, sensitive, and with socialist learnings, Josie was a good companion to her husband. She assisted him with manuscripts, and later wrote for Algerian newspapers. They had two sons, and today she lives in Algiers with them.

Fanon was appointed Head of the Psychiatric Department, Blida-Joinville Hospital in Algeria the same year. In his rounds of duty, he found the medical facilities inadequate and patients' care appalling. Amazed at seeing a nurse attending sixty-nine patients who were in straight-jackets and chained to their beds, he ordered her to release them to the great surprise of those around.[5] In place of chains and straight-jackets, Fanon introduced a more free atmosphere in which segregation depended on the relative aggressiveness of the inmates; the least potentially dangerous were allowed free movement in the wards. And by placing patients in groups of supervised activities, he offered them the opportunity to graduate from the hospital. This orientation introduced humanness in the world of the mentally ill, in the lives of those whose outlet for colonial pressures was mental derangement. Although his attempts to bring fresh ideas to the treatment of the patients were not welcomed by some of his colleagues, he continued to devote his services to his patients. His experience with patients convinced him of the scars of colonialism; and this made him resolve to see "the exploitation of man by man to cease forever on this earth."

The year 1954 saw the outbreak of the Algerian Revolution. Fanon, disgusted with the violence and inhumanity of the French colonial forces, resigned in protest, and threw his lot in with the rebels. He became an editor of the F.L.N. (*Front de Liberatione Nationale*) newspaper, *El Moudjahid,* in Tunis.

In 1956, Fanon attended the Congress of Black Writers and Artists in Paris. The meeting was a representation of the old and young among Black writers and artists. Among those attending were well-known personalities such as Aime Cesaire, Fanon's teacher, Richard Wright, Leopold Senghor, Jacques Alexis, and Alioune Diop. A major theme of the congress was the influence of French colonization on African culture. Fanon's speech[6] was an attack on French racism with regard to African culture. Fanon attended the All-African Peoples' Conference in Accra, Ghana, 1958, where he passionately pleaded for the recognition of the native African cause. He also participated in many other conferences on the destiny of Africa. Energetic and enthusiastic, he wanted to accomplish much as time was moving fast for him. He was a marked man by French colonial forces as he travelled to establish contacts for getting aid for the Algerian revolutionary front and African unity. Fortunately, he escaped with only one serious injury in a mine on the Algerian-Moroccan border in 1959. It was in this year that *L'an V de la Revolution Algerienne (a Dying Colonialism)* was published.

He was appointed the representative of the Algerian Provisional Government to Ghana in 1960. From his post here and sometimes travelling incognito, he saw to the establishment of recruiting posts for Algerian war and the transportation of military hardware. But nobody has complete control of his destiny. Fanon's exuberance was marred by leukemia.

In 1961, he flew to Rome to see Jean-Paul Sartre about his agreement to write the preface of *Les Damnes de la Terre (The Wretched of the Earth)*. They had a long conversation which Simone de Beauvoir recorded. *The Wretched of the Earth* was published that year in Paris. The book expresses Fanon's feelings about liberation and liberation movements.

Unable to get adequate medical treatment in U.S.S.R., Fanon was referred to the National Institutes of Health, Bethesda, Maryland, U.S.A. I worked part-time in this multi-complex of medical facility for the treatment of cancer and other diseases for three years, and my experience here convinced me of the prudence of Fanon's referral. But Fanon's disease was terminal. He died in December, 1961. His body was flown to Algeria where it was buried in a background of distant artillery fires.

This ends the early life of Frantz Fanon. His epitaph is best written in his own words:

> What I want to say is that death is always close by, and what's important is not to know if you can avoid it, but to know that you have done the most possible to realize your ideas . . . We are nothing on earth if we are not, first of all, slaves of a cause, the cause of the people, the cause of justice, the cause of liberty.[7]

In the following year, the Algerians gained independence. The year 1964 saw the publication of *Pour la Revolution Africaine (Toward the African Revolution)* in Paris. Our investigation aims at unravelling the undulating currents of Fanon's adventure.

PREFACE

Frantz Fanon was a humanist who eventually espoused revolutionary violence in order to relieve the oppression of the colonial system. On reading such a description, one is faced with a philosophical problem, namely, that of "consistency" or "contradiction" of the stance of his humanism in view of the fact that, in the mind of a large number of people today, revolutionary violence is contrary to genuine humanism.

Because Fanon has been portrayed by some writers as a man of violence, a rabid revolutionary without any redeeming features, the problem of reconciling his humanism with revolutionary violence is all the more acute. Lewis Coser ranked him among "the very great mythopoeists of our age," who have "created an evil myth."[1] In his discussion of social philosophers, Robert Nisbet gave Fanon as "an example of the persisting legacy of Jacobinism."[2] And J.E. Seigel claimed that "he was a man of contradictions."[3] Consequently, the point of our inquiry on Fanon's revolutionary humanism crucially lies in the critique of his use of violence.

Fanon has a vision or project of a "new humanism" in which he wants "to discover, and to love man, wherever he may be."[4] In other words, in my opinion, he projects the establishment of a genuinely universalist humanism which will include Blacks who have been denied some of the basic values of the old humanism through colonial subjugation. The problem is how to reconcile his humanism with his use of violence.

In this study, we shall see that Fanon is not an apostle of violence who has "created an evil myth" but rather that he is a man struggling to reconcile the apparent contradiction between genuine humanism and violence. In order to reconcile his humanism and his espousal of violence one must consider his conception of revolution in the light of the principle of self-defense on the part of the oppressed. Fanon attempts to achieve this reconciliation by placing humanism and violence in a dialectical tension. An attempt to describe this tension will constitute a critical thrust of this study.

Since the problem of Fanon's revolutionary humanism with regard to the use of violence is a thorny one, it appropriately dominates the first part of our study, and needs the method of elucidation by analysis of the terms used. Much confusion can be generated in a discussion of this nature if the terms are not clarified and made precise by showing in what sense they are used in a given context or discussion. We must therefore begin by analyzing some of the key terms in order to see how they are used in Fanon's revolutionary humanism. The terms that need elucidation are as follows: humanism, revolution, and violence.

Our overall method is to present Fanon's views with some background and with some critical evaluation of the issues involved in view of the argument of this study. Although Fanon's views are amenable to sociological, psychological, psychoanalytical and linguistic analysis owing to various influences on his thoughts, we shall mainly concentrate on revolutionary humanism from the philosophical perspective. We shall therefore first deal with the exposition of the terms which we have already indicated in order to provide a critical framework, then in the following chapter, consider the features of Fanon's humanism which will advance the critical analysis; then in the third chapter, discuss the crisis situation or the alienation of the oppressed or colonized which requires resolution as a human problem in the light of genuine humanism. In the fourth chapter we shall discuss the main critical framework, namely, the principle of self-defense on which to ground the justification of Fanon's espousal of violence, and thereby clear the ground for dismissing Coser's charge. Furthermore, here we shall discuss and evaluate the crucial issues of killing the innocent, the use of torture, and terrorism, because revolutionary humanism may stand or fall on such grounds. Chapter V will constitute the resolution of the problem of reconciling Fanon's humanism with violence in the light of the above principle and issues. In the chapters that follow, viz., sixth, seventh, eighth, ninth, we shall endeavor to discuss other aspects of Fanon's thoughts in order to present his whole picture. Thus, chapter six will deal with his thoughts on Africa and the world at large; chapter seven will treat of his idea of revolutionary praxis; chapter eight will constitute an important investigation of his search for socio-political ideal where non-violence begins to come into focus; and finally in chapter nine we shall conclude with some critical remarks on Fanon's venture. Let us now begin with the exposition of the terms, starting with humanism.

—*Richard C. Onwuanibe, Ph.D*

Cleveland, Ohio

ACKNOWLEDGMENTS

For permission to reprint the quotations from Frantz Fanon's works grateful acknowledgments are made to the following:

Grove Press, Inc. (New York City, U.S.A.), Granada Publishing, Ltd., (St. Albans, Hertfordshire, England) for quotations from *Black Skin, White Masks,* translated by Charles Lam Markmann; *The Wretch of the Earth,* translated by Constance Farrington; *Toward the African Revolution,* translated by Haakon Chevalier; *A Dying Colonialism,* translated by Haakon Chevalier.

Monthly Review Press for quotations from *Toward the African Revolution,* English translation, copyright ©1967.

CONTENTS

Dedication .... *v*
Biographical Notes .... *ix*
Preface ....*xv*
Acknowledgments .... *xvii*

CHAPTER   *PAGE*
I TOWARD A CRITICAL ANALYSIS 1
   1. EXPOSITION OF THE TERMS 1
     (i) Humanism 1
     (ii) Revolution 3
     (iii) Violence 6
     (iv) Force 10
     (v) Coercion 10
     (vi) Pressure 10
II FEATURES OF FANON'S HUMANISM 13
   1. HUMAN DIGNITY OR RECOGNITION 13
   2. FREEDOM 21
   3. SEARCH FOR JUSTICE, LOVE AND PEACE 23
   4. UNIVERSALIST CHARACTER 27
   5. THE EMERGENCE OF A NEW MAN 29
   6. DIALECTICAL CHARACTER 30
III THE CRISIS SITUATION:
   ALIENATION OF THE COLONIZED 35
   1. MEANING OF ALIENATION 36
   2. ALIENATION IN HEGEL AND MARX 36
   3. FANON ON THE ALIENATION
   OF THE NEGRO, THE COLONIZED 41
     (i) Alienation as Cultural Imposition: Language ... 42
     (ii) Colour Prejudice 43
     (iii) The Colonial System 45
   4. ETHICS OF COLONIAL IMPERIALISM 46
   5. THE CASE OF ALGERIA 49
IV CRITICAL PRINCIPLES:
   JUSTIFYING VIOLENCE 58
   1. FANON'S DILEMMA 58
   2. REMARKS ON VIOLENCE...................... 59

CONTENTS

3. SELF-DEFENSE 60
4. THE INNOCENT 64
   (i) Who are the Innocent? 64
   (ii) Killing the Innocent 64
5. THE PRINCIPLE OF DOUBLE EFFECT 66
6. TORTURE 73
7. THE USE OF TERROR 74
V RESOLUTION 79
VI AFRICA AND THE WORLD 95
1. AFRICAN UNITY 97
2. REPARATION FOR COLONIAL INJUSTICE 99
VII REVOLUTIONARY PRAXIS 101
   REVOLUTIONARY AGENCIES
VIII SOCIO-POLITICAL IDEAL 108
1. CRITICISM OF NATIONALIST PARTIES 108
2. DECENTRALIZATION AND SOCIALISM 110
IX CONCLUDING REMARKS 113

Biographical Notes 118
Selected Bibliography 119
   Primary Sources 119
   Secondary Sources 119
   Philosophical Works 120
   General Works 128
NOTES 128
   Preface 128
   Chapter I 128
   Chapter II 129
   Chapter III 131
   Chapter IV 134
   Chapter V 135
   Chapter VI 136
   Chapter VII 137
   Chapter VIII 138
   Chapter IX 138

Name Index 139
Subject Index 143

A CRITIQUE OF
REVOLUTIONARY HUMANISM:
FRANTZ FANON

Chapter I
TOWARD A CRITICAL ANALYSIS

1. EXPOSITION OF THE TERMS

(i) Humanism

The term "humanism" is a slippery word that today covers a watershed of opinions, attitudes, outlooks and movements centring around man. It is derived from the Latin words *"homo,"* man, and *"genus humanum,"* mankind. It also derives from *"humanitas"* which Cicero used to denote the education of man or human excellence.

Rooted in classical antiquity, humanism in the strict sense, often refers to the phenomenon of the Renaissance, which portrayed man in his potentialities, achievements and foibles as seen through the revival of classical models and values in the arts and literature. Those who prided themselves as humanists devoted themselves to the study of classical texts, to the fullest development of man with regard to actualizing the possibilities of his freedom and to counteracting whatever hinders human growth. They viewed learning not only as theoretical speculation but as having bearing on the problems of real life. Hence, they were concerned with the ethical dimension of life in order to achieve a "universal man,"[1] a well-rounded personality. The classical concept of education (*paideia*)[2] was revived as a model. It is important to note that some of the humanists were devoted to ameliorating the inhuman and unjust conditions of their time in the social and political spheres.[3]

Some humanists have given centrality to man by making him a self-creating being. Some have isolated human life from the supernatural horizon, and made human life have value and dignity by itself without reference to God. Hence, as a philosphy, humanism means to some, as Corliss Lamont put it, "a system which holds that the chief end of human life

1

is to work for the happiness of man upon this earth and within the confines of Nature that is his home."[4]

To a certain extent, humanism is a reaction against religious authority and religious conception of man and his world. However, it would be false to think of humanism only as an anti-religious movement, for European humanism has been theocentric[5] and anthropocentric; and a dialectic has often been maintained between the two by its proponents to the present day. The secularized version of humanism seems to have taken the name in such a way that a humanist is often regarded as an atheist.

Humanism has become a blanket term covering those streams of thought which aim at fostering the full development of man, that is, protecting his dignity, loving and caring for him.

Fanon uses the term "humanism" within the context of this philosophy. However, his is "a new humanism," as he proclaims, because it is a move to extend human dignity, freedom, love, care and justice to the Black man and all the oppressed, and liberate man from all forms of exploitation: that is, to really universalize these values. Thus on the first page of the introduction of his first book, *Black Skin, White Masks,* he announces his project of humanism:

> Toward a new humanism
> Understanding among men
>
> . . .
> Mankind, I believe in you
>
> . . .
> To understand and love . . . [6]

This ejaculatory passage receives explication and emphasis in his definition of man:

> Man is not merely a possibility of recapture or of negation. If it is true that consciousness is a process of transcendence, we have to see too that this transcendence is haunted by the problems of love and understanding. Man is a *Yes* that vibrates to cosmic harmonies.
>
> . . .
> *Yes* to life. *Yes* to generosity. But man is also a *No*. *No* to scorn of man. *No* to degradation of man. *No* to exploitation of man. *No* to the butchery of what is most human in man: freedom. Man's behavior is not only reactional. And there is always resentment in a *reaction*. Nietzsche had already pointed that out in *The Will to Power*. To educate man to be *actional*, preserving in all his relation his respect for the basic values that constitute

a human world, is the prime task of him who, having taken thought, prepares to act.[7]

By way of interpretation, these passages show that the essence of Fanon's humanism is the establishment of the human world characterized by the basic values of recognition, justice, freedom, love, understanding and peace. Although these basic values naturally tend to achieve this purpose of building a human world, they are frustrated by antagonistic forces which tend to the alienation of man. Yet man's inborn negativity strives to overcome these forces in self and social realization. These features of Fanon's humanism need further elucidation by way of analysis. In my opinion, Fanon's humanism should be considered within the critical framework of genuine or universalist humanism. A genuinely universalist humanism is geared to protecting human rights, such as rights to life, freedom, and property, and to respecting every man, even the enemy, and to loving every man. Fanon's "new humanism" seems to be a project toward this. We shall consider this in greater detail in the next chapter. We must now consider the second key term of our investigation, namely, revolution.

(ii) Revolution

In order to provide a critical framework for understanding Fanon's conception of revolution, it is relevant to indicate briefly the etymological background and some issues of revolution, because some scholars are not agreed on what changes and conflicts we may call revolutionary.

Revolution is not a univocal term. It is difficult to define it, because revolutions are historical and complex phenomena to be considered in the context of a particular social and political milieu, whereas definitions are often generalizations. We are concerned here with the socio-political meaning of the term and not with the term as denoting scientific[8] and economic phenomena, because Fanon's conception of revolution is within the socio-political context. From a historical point of view, every revolution is unique, and so defies any attempts to lump all together. However, there are indications of family resemblance, which allow for generalization.

In his study of revolution, Peter Calvert refers to the ancient Egyptian experience of rebellion during the period when the northern and southern kingdoms were united (C. 3200 B.C. and thereafter) as the origin of the idea of revolution. The Egyptians fought a war of national liberation against the Hyksos ('Shepherd Kings') who invaded and ruled them with terror for more than four hundred years. Their rebellion against alien rule made a great impact on the ancient world. As Calvert puts it, "Clearly the identification of the concept of rebellion is an important step on the way to an identification of revolution."[9] He points out that the impact of the Egyptian experience on the ancient world had great influence on Aristotle's analysis of the Greek experience of revolutionary change.[10] The concept of rebellion which leads to the recognition of revolution is therefore not new.[11]

In defining revolution, Aristotle located it in the spectrum of change (*metabole*) within types of governments:

> Here then, so to speak, are opened the very springs and fountains of revolution; and hence arise two sorts of changes in governments; the one affecting the constitution, when men seek to change from an existing form into some other, for example, from democracy into oligarchy, and from oligarchy into democracy, or from either of them into constitutional government or aristocracy, and conversely; the other not affecting the constitution, when, without disturbing the form of government, whether oligarchy, or monarchy, or any other, they try to get the administration into their own hands.[12]

Aristotle considered change from one political arrangement to another as cyclical such that the death knell of one form of political organization sounded the birth of another. It is important to note that he treated mostly of political revolution, that is, the displacement of one form of government by another by political protagonists. However, he did not stress the social aspect of such a revolution; that is, he did not stress how the displacement of one form of government by another is also a means of solving the social problems of class structure, inequality, discrimination and poverty. Fanon stresses both aspects. Karl Marx, on the other hand, stresses the social aspect. Another important point to bear in mind is that, for Aristotle, violence is not an essential ingredient of revolution. To him, revolution can be accomplished "by force and by fraud."[13]

The idea of violence was introduced into the concept of revolution when Polybius, the Greek historian, translated *metabole* into Latin as *commutatio* (change in the form of a cycle).[14] The political arena of Republican Rome was not without its violent aspects, since violence was regarded by many as a proper expediency with the important proviso, "that the victims did not have their *dignities infringed.*"[15] The problem here, I think, is how this can be done in a particular situation. Accordingly, in the Roman political scene, desire for revolutionary change *(cupido novarum rerum)* had the coloration of violence.[16]

Many a student of revolution has located violence in the concept of revolution. Charles Ellwood considers revolution to be marked with "abrupt violent changes" in human affairs.[17] Johnson Chalmers defines revolution as "the acceptance of violence in order to bring about change."[18] Harry Eckstein who designates revolution as "internal war" locates its essence in the "attempts to change by violence, or threat of violence, a government's policies, rules or organization."[20]

Fanon follows this tradition of considering revolution as a violent phenomenon, though, I think, it is debatable whether it is always so. Eugene Kameka is right in putting it thus:

> A sharp, sudden change in the social location of political power, expressing itself in the radical transformation of the processes of government, of the foundations of sovereignty or legitimacy and of the conception of the social order. Such transformations, it has usually been believed, could not normally occur without violence, but if they did, they could still, though bloodless, be revolutions.[21]

Revolution, I think, is the attempt to change or break away from the social or political structure by challenging or over-throwing the established authority, legitimate or illegitimate, by violence or otherwise. Although violence may not be an essential ingredient of revolution, revolution is to be located within the spectrum of change and conflict. For example, a revolution could be brought about by an army coup in conflict with the *de facto* or *de jure* authority without bloody violence, but also by a threat of violence or by strategy. The element of violence introduces the problem of justifying a particular revolution which is violent in view of genuine humanism. This is the problem of Fanon.

According to Fanon, revolution is a process of liberation, of decolonizing the colonial system, or challenging the colonial power by violence on the part of the natives in a bid for justice, liberty and freedom. It is a process of gaining national independence. It involves, to some extent, a revolving back to the precolonial history of the colonized which has been disrupted by the colonial forces, the restoration of their values which have been inferiorized, the recreation of the colonized as they meet the challenge to their humanity, and the re-ordering of the social and political structure as the people forge their new nation.[22] To him, a revolutionary is one who fights against oppression and devotes himself to new socio-political arrangements in which freedom is realized.

Fanon's concept of revolution accords, to some extent, to the notion of revolution as a restoration, a reactionary movement of Locke's day, and also to the notion of revolution as a break with the existing socio-political structure, here the colonial structure. It is a movement for the re-direction of the history of the colonized. In other words, it accords with the modern notion of revolution as a means of using violence "to constitute an altogether different form of government, to bring about the formation of a new body politic where the liberation from oppression aims at least at the constitution of freedom."[23] Thus Fanon announces the process of decolonization or revolution in the colonial system as a violent phenomenon:

> National liberation, national renaissance, the restoration of nationhood to the people, commonwealth ... whatever may be the headings used or the new formulas introduced, decolonization is always a violent phenomenon ... decolonization is quite simply the replacing of a certain "species" of men by another "species" of men. Without any period of transition, there is a total, complete, and absolute substitution ...
>
> ... To tell the truth, the proof of success lies in a whole social structure being changed from bottom up.[24]

Since, according to Fanon, violence is a necessary ingredient of the colonial revolution, he faces the problem of the compatibility of violence with his project of establishing a genuine humanism. Hence, we shall now discuss his conception of violence in order to avoid the confusion generated by mixing it up with other notions, such as force, coercion and pressure.

(iii) Violence

In dealing with the problem of defining violence in view of Fanon's revolutionary humanism, it is important to note that we are going to consider violence in the context of human action. In this context, a person does violence to another person or property; a group does violence to another group or property. One suffers violence, or is a victim of violence. We shall leave out the consideration of the term "violence" as applied to animals, though we may refer to it in this sense.

To understand Fanon's notion of violence, it is important,

of course, to know what violence is. A flood of literature on violence has appeared within the decade, which indicates the significance and perplexity of the problem of violence today. Not all agree on the definition of violence.

Violence, like revolution, is one of those troublesome terms which are so charged with emotion that its definition may depend on which side of the fence one belongs. Thus, a definition may prejudge the issue. For example, in a legalistic sense violence is defined as the "illegitimate force or unauthorized use of force to effect decisions against the will or desire of others."[25] Here emphasis is placed on legitimacy rather than on the objective injury done on the human person. According to this definition murder is distinguished as an act of violence from capital punishment because it is "unauthorized" while the latter is "authorized" by a legitimate state and therefore is not an act of violence. Pressed further, the legalistic definition pushes the problem of violence to the problem of the legitimacy of a particular state since legitimacy may be acquired by a *de facto* government by prescription even though it is not *de jure;* that is, by maintaining power over a period of time, it acquires recognition, politically speaking. The legalistic definition is too narrow for a critical examination of the issue of violence with regard to the objective injury done to the human person. The aspect of objective injury done to the human person is important in considering the revolutionary humanism of Fanon's stance. Both the physical and psychological dimensions of violence need to be taken into account.

In his study of violence, Ronald B. Miller defines it as an act by A that

1) involves great force
2) is in itself capable of injuring, damaging or destroying and
3) is done with the intent of injury, damaging, or destroying B (a being), or O (an inanimate object), where the damage or destruction of an object by A is only an act of violence when it was not done with the intention of doing something of value for the objects' owners.[26]

This definition emphasizes the element of physical injury or its possibility as the consequence of the force applied to the being or object. However, it is inadequate in that it takes account only of the physical aspect of violence and not the psychological aspect, which, as we have already mentioned, should be included. In this connection let us consider Robert Audi's definition:

Violence is the physical attack upon, or the vigorous physical abuse of, vigorous physical struggle against, a person or animal; or the highly vigorous psychological attack upon a person or animal; or the highly vigorous, or incendiary, or malicious and vigorous, destruction or damaging of property or potential property.[27]

This definition is interesting in that it attempts to take into account various aspects of violence; that is, its physical, psychological and ethical aspects. Although physical violence may have psychological effect, psychological violence may be induced without physical contact. For example, when a man vilifies another man or woman to the point of causing a mental breakdown. Psychological violence has not often received the attention it deserves because it is not regarded as constituting a paradigmatic case of violence. However, I think, it is of great relevance in dealing with the concept of violence at the social and political levels, and in the colonial context which Fanon describes. At the social and political levels psychological violence may take the form of institutionalized discrimination on grounds of race, colour, religion and sex. The victim of racial prejudice may suffer the torture of inferiority complex to the breaking point. For example, the discrimination against Black Americans and other minority groups is a strong case of psychological violence. In this sense, the colonial system is ridden with psychological violence. Fanon describes in great detail this form of violence.

Along this line, some of those who reject limiting the definition of violence to the physical aspect, prefer to consider violence as essentially "anything that obstructs the legitimate functioning of a person."[28] In this sense, it would include a wide range of items such as causing physical pain, disablement, killing, deprivation of freedom, and of the opportunity for self-realization. Here the objective conditions or structures which lead to the alienation of a person or a group are included in the sense that they are due to the failure of the powers-that-be to act, or to direct intentions of the exploiting group, as in the case of segregation and apartheid.

Although the above definition may serve as a working framework for dealing with the general problem of alienation and violence in the colonial system, it is however too broad for discussing Fanon's use of revolutionary violence. In view of making a critique of Fanon's use of revolutionary violence, we shall mean by "violence" great force which is capable of injuring, damaging or destroying a man or property, or intensive psychological attack or incendiary attack on a person or property. The intention of the perpetrator is important since we are considering violence in the context of human action. This definition will include disablement, torture, terror, killing, bombing and shooting. These will form the elements in the critique of Fanon's revolutionary humanism.

It is relevant here to distinguish violence from mere force and coercion because some writers sometimes conflate them because of the fact that they are related. Fanon often does this. This is why, I think, Barbara Deming has suggested that whenever Fanon uses the word "violence," one may "with the exception of a very few passages" substitute "radical and uncompromising action. [29] She would take this to mean at times "nonviolent action," which, I think, would mean force or even coercion. It is true that Fanon sometimes interchanges the terms "violence" and "force" but not always, as one may read from one among many passages in his work:

> The naked truth of decolonization evokes for us the searing bullets and blood stained knives which emanate from it. For if the last shall be first, this will only come to pass after a murderous and decisive struggle between the two protagonists (i.e. the colonizer and the colonized). That affirmed intention to place the last at the head of things, and to make them climb at a pace (too quickly), some say, the well-known steps which characterize an organized society, can only triumph if we use all means to turn the scale, including, of course, that of violence.[30]

The above passage shows that Fanon's use of the term "violence" includes killing and shooting, that is, great force which is capable of injuring, damaging or destroying a man.

To Fanon, violence also means struggle which is expressed in uncompromising action. Thus he writes:

> Violence alone, violence committed by the people, violence *organized* and educated by its leaders, makes possible for the masses to understand social truth and the key to them. Without that *struggle*,[31] without that *knowledge of the practice of action*, there's nothing but fancy dress parade . . . a few reforms at the top . . . and down there at the bottom an undivided mass . . . endlessly marking time.[32]

Here, I think, violence may connote force, which may or may not result in injury. Here it is relevant to discuss the distinction between violence, force, coercion and pressure in order to get a clearer idea of what Fanon means by violence.[33]

(iv) Force

We can speak of "force" in general as that which has power, influence or impact. In the context of human relationship and action, we can "force someone to do something," and "use force" to accomplish an aim, or "forcibly do something." In this sense, force is any action done for the purpose of physically overpowering a person or an object. When the overpowering results in injury, or is intended for injury or destruction, it becomes violence. But force does not imply violence as in the case where a brother gently removes a younger brother to prevent him from going near a deep pool.

(v) Coercion

We may also distinguish violence from coercion. To coerce a person is to use force to make a person do something other than he wishes, or to bend him to one's wishes. A person can be coerced by being incapacitated in the sense that he is made incapable of acting physically. Coercion can be accomplished by using violence, that is, force which results in injury. Someone can also be coerced by being subjected to suffering, to the threat of violence, to the threat of force or by being a victim of burdens. Revolutionary violence may take the form of social and political coercion.

(vi) Pressure

In this connection, we may distinguish violence from pressure. Often a person may do something under persuasion which is at the rational level of discussion. But beyond persuasion is pressure which borders on coercion. To put pressure on a person is not to deal personally with him, but to use material or psychological means to bend him to one's wishes; however, the person is allowed a self-respecting legitimate option as a way out. It differs from coercion in that it does not allow the opponent to suffer without a legitimate alternative.

An overall consideration of Fanon's use of the term "violence," I think, reveals that he uses it to refer to various aspects or stages of the struggle for liberation and national independence on the part of the oppressed or colonized. It expresses an aspect of human negativity, which affirms the dignity of each person irrespective of colour or race, and a positive response to humanizing influences, and also the negation in practice of whatever alienates or dehumanizes man. In this sense, violence is a form of struggle, uncompromising action. Violence also, to Fanon, denotes armed force for liberating the national territory and culture in the cause of freedom from the conquest and war force of the colonial power.

An important aspect of Fanon's conception of violence that must not be overlooked is his view that violence has cleansing and therapeutic effects. He writes:

> At the level of individuals, *violence is a cleansing force.* It frees the native from his inferiority complex and from his despair and inaction; it makes him fearless and restores his self-respect. Even if the armed struggle has been symbolic and the nation is demolished through a rapid movement of de-colonization, the people have the time to see that the libera-tion has been the business of each and all and that the leader has no special merit. From thence comes that type of aggres-sive reticence with regard to the machinery of protocol which young governments quickly show. When the people have taken violent part in the national liberation they will allow no one to set themselves up as 'liberators.' They show themselves to be jealous of the results of their action and take good care not to place their future, their destiny or the fate of their country in the hands of a living god. Yesterday they were irresponsible; today they mean to understand everything and make all deci-sions. *Illuminated by violence, the consciousness of the people rebels against any pacification.* From now on the demagogues, the opportunists and the magicians have a difficult task. The action which has thrown men into a hand-to-hand struggle confers upon the masses a voracious taste for the concrete. The attempt at mystification becomes, in the long run, prac-tically impossible.[34]

In interpreting the above message, it is necessary to keep in mind our discussion of how Fanon uses the term "violence" to designate different aspects of the struggle for decolonization, and of human negativity. Fanon prizes struggle as a means of expressing one's manhood and ability to assume the respon-sibility for one's or a people's life. To be "illuminated by vio-lence" is to be aware of one's responsibility for one's struggle in the cause of freedom, the most important part of us. One as-pect of the "cleansing force" of violence is that the individual or people shed their inferiority complex in the struggle. The people now feel that they are capable of self-determination, and the individual who has taken part in the liberation move-ment has a sense of self-respect for asserting his human dig-nity against the challenge to his humanity. As he put it:

> Decolonization brings a natural rhythm into existence, introduced by new men, and with it a new language and a new humanity, the "thing" which has been colonized becomes man during the same process by which it frees itself.[35]

Violence, in a certain sense, according to Fanon, is equated with absolute form of the praxis of decolonization. Through revolutionary action the crushing burden of. the oppressed is uplifted. Decolonization, as Fanon describes it, "transforms spectators crushed with their inessentiality into privileged actors, with the gradiose glare of history's flood lights upon them."[36] Man is the maker of history. During the process of decolonization the colonized make their history.

However, the interpretation of violence as struggle does not exclude the traumatic elements of violence with regard to acts of violence, such as, killing, burning, shooting, bombing, mutilation, which the liberation struggle may entail. As Irene L. Gendzier has pointed out, "to justify violence as part of the need for armed struggle in a process of national liberation is one thing; to justify individual acts of violence in the belief that they cleanse those who act, is something quite different."[37]

Realistic studies of wars of liberation show the "anguish of freedom." The Battle of Algiers took a heavy toll of lives. It was a defensive battle on the part of the colonized. It may be argued that the cleansing force of violence in the war of independence can be seen in the fact that the participants are consoled that they are not suffering in vain because of the hope of national independence in the long run. But this does not eliminate the physical and mental suffering of the dead and wounded. The "anguish of freedom" becomes poignant when the sacrifice made appears to be too high a price to be paid. The idea of a "cleaning force of violence" appears to be mixed and confused, and Fanon has not simplified the issue by using the term "violence" to denote different aspects of the struggle, and of the conflict.

By providing a critical framework of background and relevant issues, the preceding exposition of the terms has sharpened the focus of our investigation of the problem of consistency in Fanon's humanism. In order to advance our critical analysis it is important to discuss the features of Fanon's humanism in detail.

Chapter II
FEATURES OF FANON'S HUMANISM

Fanon's project of "a new humanism" is a reaction to the fact that the colonial powers and colonizers did not accord full humanity to the colonized. He was dismayed by the fact that they proclaimed the values of human dignity, freedom, justice, love and peace, but did not extend them to their other human counterpart, the colonized or oppressed.[1]

However, instead of despairing of man, Fanon decided to struggle in the form of colonial revolution in order to universalize the humanistic values to reach Black people. In order to advance the critical appreciation of his revolutionary humanism, as we have indicated in the preceding chapter, we shall consider the salient features of his humanism, namely (1) the value of human dignity or recognition, (2) the value of freedom, (3) the values of justice, love and peace, (4) its universalist character, (5) the emergence of a new man, and (6) its dialectical character. In considering these features, we shall elaborate on them with relevant illustrations and critical framework and interpretation.

1. HUMAN DIGNITY OR RECOGNITION

The dictum of Socrates that "unexamined life is not wroth living,"[2] and his advice that men should know themselves show that human life is of great value and is worthy of care. Fanon follows this advice in his investigative study of the life of the Black or colonized in relation to that of the White and the colonizers.

As Fanon points out, the history of mankind can be summed up as a history of the struggle of individual and peoples to achieve human dignity or recognition. In other words, as a bird's eye view of history shows, human dignity has suffered from lack of universalization, from deprivation, and at times, from attack. We may add here by way of illustration that Aristotle's reduction of some people to the status of slaves by nature because they did not participate fully in reason,[3] and therefore were excluded from the good life came under fire from the Sophists and Stoics, who by infusing the liberal elements into the Greek concept of man, universalized the notion of human dignity to extend to the non-Greeks (barbarians) by their concept of racial equality. Antiphon, a Sophist, for example, challenged the social distinctions which the Greeks took for granted. He appealed to nature which makes no distinctions with regard to our basic needs and their satisfaction as the basis of equality of men. Thus he writes:

> The sons of noble fathers we respect and look up to, but those from humble homes we neither respect nor look up to. In this we behave to one another like barbarians, since by nature we are all made to be alike in all respects, both barbarians and Greeks. This can be seen from the needs which all men have. They can all be provided in the same way by all men, and in all this none of us is marked off as either barbarian or Greek; for we all breathe the air with our mouth and nostrils and eat with our hands? . . .[4]

Since the exclusively conservation Greek mind did not universalize the possession of reason, it is significant that Antiphon switched from reason to nature. Here we see a glimmer of the concept of person and the respect for the human person based on nature; for nature is common to all without any essential distinction of high and low birth, or between various races, even though there may be cultural differences. Cultures may be equally good, though different. Antiphon was, in fact, putting the Greeks to task for paying too much attention to a man's race or descent instead of thinking of the community of mankind based on nature.

Antiphon seems to be saying that, by underrating the non Greeks as *barbaroi,* stupid and uncivilized, the Greeks were going against what nature has made as good as themselves, and which they had failed to acknowledge through ignorance, and so would be the ones who were really uncivilized. Provocative and caustic, Antiphon's criticism in favour of the egalitarian spirit had no small impact on raising the Greek consciousness to universalize their concept of what is human. Although slaves at this period might have the recognition of law forbidding "an act of *hybris* against slaves as well as citizens,"[5] they were, at bottom, regarded as chattel. However, a wave against slavery rippled with the theme which Alcidamas, a pupil of Gorgias, eloquently put thus: "God has set all men free; nature has made no man a slave."[6]

The logic of slavery, I think, is that it is not easy to enslave a man unless he has been depersonalized and "thingified." War victims were often enslaved. The process of victimization in war is a process of depersonalization. Unfortunately, the degradation of the war victims was often extended to the whole race of the victims.

Along the line of the above criticism, we may also add that the Stoics who based human worth on man's sharing of reason, the "spark of the divine," saw in the slave the spark of the divine which is in all nature, and which gave him human dignity. The impact of this on the Greek exclusiveness did not bring about some change without some crisis, in aristocratic values, and in the interpretation of accepted notions on which social distinctions and prejudices are based.

We may also say that the acceptance of the *barbaroi* with respect as human beings might have been a painful experience to the conservative elements who would like to maintain the *status quo*. This is the crisis, I think, of what may be called classical humanism in the effort to universalize the respect for the human person to include non-Greeks.

The point of the above illustration is to show that the same kind of crisis can be observed as a historical phenomenon where subject peoples attempt to win human respect from the "masters." And I think that this dialectic of the master and subject seems to be a constant of the history of civilization in the conquest of human recognition, which essentially characterizes an authentically universalist humanism to which, I think, Fanon is committed. Difficulties arise when the crisis issues in a revolution.

Fanon is in the tradition of those who want to universalize the concept of human dignity with regard to the relationship of Blacks and Whites. He sees the "Black problem" as the problem of recognition; and in human relationship, he points up that he has a fundamental right to demand human behaviour from others.[7] The importance of the problem of recognition can be gauged by the extensive attention which he devotes to it in his first book, *Black Skin, White Masks*. It is a central issue in his revolutionary humanism, because recognition is at a markedly human level, the bedrock of an authentic human relation. It draws an irreversible line, I think, between a human existence and a "thingified" existence.

Fanon approaches the problem of recognition or human dignity from the postive and negative viewpoints: however, he dwells more on the negative side in view of the alienation and disalienation of the Black and White.

Fanon's concept of human recognition, to a large extent, derives from that of Hegel. He comments on Hegel's concept of recognition. Hegel has a dynamic concept of man in which the desire for recognition and freedom are essential:

> Self-consciousness exists in itself and for itself, in that, and by the fact that it exists for another self-consciousness; that is to say, it is only by being acknowledged or "recognized."[8]

To comment, man as a striving being means the desire to be recognized as unique; that is, in the words of Kant, "never to be used as a means except when he is at the same time an end."[9] The human makes demands. According to Hegel, each person desires the desire of the other, to be recognized as unique. However, recognition rests on success in a struggle to death, though death does not actually occur. Recognition is a correlative of freedom. Recognition and freedom are high qualities of life. In throwing down the gauntlet, the one who defeats the other becomes the master, and the other a slave.[10]

Hegel maintains that it is by risking one's life for recognition that freedom is achieved. Freedom involves saying No to the objectification of oneself, to the reduction of oneself to the status of a "thingified existence." According to Hegel, the slave is what he is because he clings to mere life self-existence, and fails to risk his life in favour of recognition. Even though, as an individual human reality, "he may be recognized as a person; but he has not attained the truth of this recognition as an independent self-consciousness."[11] The struggle to death, however, cancels true independence for him. The master somehow excels by taking the risk of his life, by his victory. However, in Hegel's view, the slave has a chance; he works himself up by his service for fear of the master; he is in touch with reality by labour through which he transforms matter into useful products which are enduring symbols of himself, of his personality; for a man expresses himself in his work. The master, on the other hand, goes down in the scale because he loses touch with reality. His victory is shortlived. He has only a negative action on things produced by the slave to satisfy his wants: consumption of products is pure negation.

The important stage of the dialectic, Hegel holds, occurs

when the master recognizes that, in fact, for all his domination, he is dependent on the slave for his existence. The master's freedom is merely abstract, and not one in reality. The scale of the dialectic tips in favour of the slave. The point here is that each needs the other. Self-consciousness, Hegel says, can only be achieved through the recognition of another self-consciousness. It is through their mutual recognition that freedom is achieved by each: "They recognize themselves as mutually recognizing each other."[12] Thus, the relationship of master and slave is transcended by a higher form of consciousness, self-consciousness in which mutual recognition of the human is possible.

Fanon takes over Hegel's dynamic concept of man as desire for recognition but rejects the ultimate description of the relation of the colonial people and the colonial powers, or the relation of Whites and Blacks only within the dialectic of the master and slave.[13] He agrees with Hegel on the fundamental desire in man for recognition and its reciprocal character. He writes:

At the foundation of Hegelian dialectic there is an absolute reciprocity that must be emphasized. It is in the degree to which I go beyond my own immediate being that I apprehend the existence of the other as a natural and more than natural reality. If I close the circuit, if I prevent the accomplishment of movement in two directions, I keep the other within himself. Ultimately, I deprive him even of this being-for-itself. The only means of breaking this vicious circle that throws back on myself is to restore to the other, through mediation and recognition, his human reality which is different from natural reality. The other has to perform the same operation.[14]

Hence, Fanon maintains that the creation of the human world is the creation of reciprocal recognition and freedom. Unfortunately, as he points out, the other may be reluctant to recognize me, and so opposes me. The opposition may involve a savage struggle in which one "is willing to accept the convulsions of death, invincible dissolution."[15] Hence, Fanon prizes struggle for recognition and freedom where conflict arises. Thus he echoes Hegel by saying:

Thus human reality in itself can be achieved only through conflict and through the risk that conflict implies. This risk means that I go beyond life toward a supreme good.[16]

This struggle for recognition, Fanon thinks, is necessary where there is a challenge to one's humanity. It is at this level

17

that he sees the difference between the master and slave in Hegel's dialectic and the relationship between the White and Black, and the colonizer and the colonized. As Fanon points out, the slave in Hegel's analysis, is not turned to the master in an aspiration to take the place of the master but only aspires to a lower kind of recognition of service, which is not grounded on true independence and freedom; whereas the Black man or the colonized man in his relation to the White man or the colonizer wants to be accorded human dignity grounded on independence and freedom.

However, Fanon makes the point that recognition does not always depend on struggle. Historically speaking, some slaves have been freed by their masters without a fight. Fanon contends that the Negro slave (French Negro) has not had a challenge to his humanity: he has been sealed "in the inessentiality of servitude."[17] Since he has not fought for his freedom, he has no memory of the "anguish of liberty,"[18] the price of freedom. The times he fought, he fought for White liberty and White justice. We may say here that the French Negro is in an ambiguous situation since he is still regarded as inferior even though he thinks that he is "French." He will continue to receive paternalistic taps on the shoulder. As Fanon perceptively observes, the former slave needs a challenge to his humanity. For the Negro the achievement of the recognition and freedom will require a struggle, and that struggle begins when he appreciates the challenge to his humanity. He will rebel to assert his existence and the existence of his fellow Negroes: he will say, "I rebel, therefore we are."

The history of the world for the most part, Fanon believes, as we have seen, is the history of men's struggle for dignity. He urges men enslaved and oppressed to join with the peoples who are already sovereign to demolish the colonial system which opposes the realization of genuine humanism.[19]

Fanon's conception of struggle in the effort to achieve recognition also derives from his psychoanalytic studies. Psychoanalytic studies have shown the importance of conflict in the development of a child's personality. The time that the child is able to say "No" is the time he is able to assume the responsibility for his life.[20] However, it is debatable whether the atmosphere of conflict makes for love and peace which are human tendencies. Here, we see the pivotal point of Fanon's humanism in the duality of human negativity which Fanon denotes as Yes and No. This duality is reflected in his search for recognition through revolution. Can this duality be maintained with regard to the use of violence without contradiction? We shall attempt to examine this question in greater detail in the fourth and fifth chapters.

At this point, we may consider further by way of critical elucidation some concrete situations which show a lack of human recognition, or show its appreciation. A foggy vision of human dignity or lack of universalizing respect for the human person to include all men may result, in moments of crisis, in acts of dehumanization, that is, in acts that are disruptive of human dignity. Acts such as brain-washing, unqualified torturing, killing the innocent, using a person as a guinea pig for experiments without his consent, mutilating a person in such a way that it may result in loss of sexuality without his consent, considering a person as subhuman and using him as a piece of property as in slave labour, denying a person the right to property or subjecting him to expropriation without just cause are acts that lack respect for the dignity of the human person. These constitute acts of violence. The problem which we shall deal with later is whether a humanist of Fanon's stance can justify them without self-contradiction. The treatment of the Jews by the Nazis resulted in acts of dehumanization. Deprived of citizenship, and later of all civil rights, they were put in concentration camps where they were tortured, dehumanized, and executed. The lynching of Negroes for no just cause, and their segregation on grounds that they are subhuman, and therefore regarded as slaves without rights constitute acts of dehumanization. The Moscow trials and subsequent purges were dehumanizing: The men involved were made victims of ideological ends without fair trial.

Respect for the human person can be shown in various life situations, where right to self-fulfillment is not stifled. Examples of such situations would be when an adult gives a child the opportunity to express himself or herself by paying attention to what the child is saying; when the child is given the opportunity of education; when you enter into a group and are not brushed aside; when you are accepted and not merely tolerated; when the teacher is sensitive to the thought of the student; when prisoners are not subject to animal treatment; when men and women are not barred from equal opportunity because of sex, race, or colour; when the unborn is defended from attacks (unjust abortion) and is given the opportunity for self-fulfillment.

In the last example, what is at stake is whether the unborn is regarded not merely as a physical growth in the womb which is regarded as part of the mother but as a human being potentially on the way to development and fulfillment with rights to life, even though in some cases there are possibilities of its being deformed. Respect is due to a deformed baby.

Although it is doubtful as to what stage the fetus can be regarded as a person, it is ethically sound to give it the benefit of the doubt even in cases where its viability or deformity is in doubt, or in cases where the life of the mother is at stake. The following case is in point. There was a pregnant woman in a general hospital in the United States of America. She was sick and some of her children were affected at birth by her disease. Her doctor told her that her baby in the womb had a ninety percent chance of being deformed if allowed to be born. So he recommended abortion (therapeutic abortion?). The woman agonized over this because her husband wanted the baby. In one of my visits, I suggested that she should allow the baby to be born. However, she allowed the doctor to perform the abortion. When I came to see her afterward she looked depressed. Why? The doctor in the process of performing the abortion found out that the baby had a ninety percent chance of being born a normal baby. But it was too late to reverse the process. In a case where the life of the mother is at stake respect for the human life of the unborn demands that every necessary effort be made to save both.

Since every man is worthy of respect because he is of intrinsic value, in dealing with individuals and groups, one man's life is to be considered to him as another man's life to him. Each is to be given the opportunity of developing according to his potentials for a fulfilled life. Although there are differences in terms of physical strength and mental ability, each person can be happy within his own interests which are made possible by differences in ability. They complement one another with regard to what each can contribute toward the well-being of society. At the human level, all men and women are equal in that they have intrinsic value in themselves because each is endowed with reason, freedom and physical qualities which make each a centre of life oriented toward self-fulfillment, and co-operation with others for the achievement of the common good. Each man is an end in himself, and should not be treated as a mere means for the achievement of other aims. It is the aim of genuine humanism, I think, to protect and enhance the value of human life and dignity.

In the next chapter we shall consider the alienation of the colonized or oppressed in the colonial system which Fanon describes as a systematic negation of human dignity. This is the seed of the contradiction in the colonial system and the seed of its dialectical replacement. We must now consider the second feature of Fanon's humanism, namely, freedom.

2. Freedom

Linked with the problem of recognition or dignity is the problem of freedom. Fanon espouses the cause of human freedom. His revolutionary humanism is basically a process of liberation and freedom.

Fanon's conception of human freedom was influenced by Hegel who maintains that freedom constitutes the essential feature of the Spirit,[17] and by existentialist thought which expresses human freedom in self-creativity. To Fanon, recognition goes together with freedom. Thus, he writes:

> I find myself suddenly in the world and I recognize that I have one right alone; That of demanding human behavior from the other. One duty alone: That of not renouncing my freedom through choice.

> I am not a prisoner of history. I should not seek there the meaning of my destiny. I should constantly remind myself that the real leap consists in introducing invention into existence. In the world through which I travel, I am endlessly creating myself. I am a part of Being to the degree that I go beyond it. And, through a private problem, we see the outline of the problemn of Action.

> No attempt must be made to encase man, for it is his destiny to be set free.[22]

> The body of history does not determine a single one of my actions. I am my own foundation and it is by going beyond the historical instrumental hypothesis that I will initiate the cycle of my freedom.[23]

To comment, although the above passages ring with a kind of existentialist abandon with regard to being one's "own foundation," they show how Fanon was committed to the promotion of human freedom in his new humanism. From the negative point of view, the promotion of freedom will consist of removing or destroying obstacles to freedom. One of the major obstacles to freedom is slavery and its consequences. In the effort to be free where there is or has been slavery, one would have to break with the past. Accordingly, Fanon makes the point that the Negro must free himself from the vindictiveness of the past with reference to the relation of the Black and White.

According to him, the Negro must be freed from the "moral anguish in the face of the massiveness of the past," and from "tons of chains, storms of blows, rivers of expectoration"[24] which come from slavery. Hence, Fanon would not be bogged down and be "the slave of the slavery that dehumanized my ancestors."[25]

Since the spirit of revenge destroys the chances of reconciliation and authentic birth of a free man, Fanon wants Blacks and Whites to free themselves from the encumbrances of the past, from being locked in a world of retroactice reparation. However, he does not leave unrecognized the fact of the disasters of inhumanity of the past:

> The disaster of the man of color lies in the fact that he was enslaved. The disaster and the inhumanity of the white man lie in the fact that somewhere he has killed man.[26]

However, the project of authentic humanism must be launched so that:

> the tool never possesses the man. That the enslavement of man by man must cease forever. That is, of one by another. That it is possible for me to discover and love man, wherever he may be. The Negro is not. Any more than the white man. Both must turn their backs on the inhuman voices which were those of their respective ancestors in order that authentic communication be possible. Before it can adopt a positive voice, freedom requires an effort at disalienation.

> Was not my freedom not given me then in order to build the world of You? At the conclusion of this study, I want the world to recognize with me the open door of every consciousness.[27]

These passages show that Fanon believes strongly in freedom with responsibility. It is a liberative freedom. Freedom can be misused in acts of injustice. One of the greatest acts of injustice is slavery; that is, the deprivation of one's freedom, the most important part of us. However, freedom with responsibility makes it possible for correcting acts of injustice and inhumanity; in other words, a responsible effort must be made by both the Black and the White in the disalienation and liberation of man. This will involve the recognition of the rights of peoples to self-determination. National independence is a major step toward real freedom on the part of the colonized. This brings us to Fanon's search for justice, love and peace.

3. SEARCH FOR JUSTICE, LOVE AND PEACE

As a humanist, Fanon was confronted with the problem of maintaining justice in the colonial system and in the world at large. In order to provide a critical reference for evaluating Fanon's search for justice, I think, it is necessary to discuss briefly the problem of justice.

How to define and maintain justice constitutes a basic problem in socio-political philosophy. The question is when is a society or political arrangement just. Since men are born free and equal, the problem is how to justify the rule of one man or group by another, or to find social and political arrangements in which freedom, equality and protection are maintained at the maximum.

The principle of justice is to give to each person or group, whether weak or strong what is his or their due and to demand the contribution of each on the basis of equal consideration.[28] What is due is often expressed in a right which is determined by law. If a person has a right to have or do something, others have the duty to respect that claim on the balance of equal protection.

Equality is an essential constituent of the principle of justice. However, "equality" of justice presents a problem,[29] since it consists of reconciling a common standard of treatment with relevant differences of individuals considered on the basis of merits and demerits. Individuals can be considered, on the one hand, as human beings with intrinsic value, in which case they are the same and entitled to respect, and have the right to life, freedom and property; and on the other hand, they are unequal on the basis of merits and demerits. In other words, the principle of justice combines the egalitarian and meritorious elements. As Plato rightly points up: "For when equality is given to unequals the result is inequality, unless due measure is applied."[30]

As Gregory Vlastos rightly puts it: "An egalitarian concept of justice may admit of just inequalities without inconsistency, if and only if, it provides grounds for equal human rights which are also grounds for unequal rights of other sorts."[31] Differential treatment of individuals should not encroach on the dignity and human rights of others. The problem here is how to determine what the relevant grounds for differential treatment of individuals are. If the determination is not to be arbitrary, the differential treatment must be based on "just making considerations or principles."[32] Irrelevant factors should not be introduced. For example, in selecting persons for jobs requiring some specific skill the colour of skin is irrelevant.

A society is just if it gives each person his or her due by respecting his or her human rights or civil rights, by allocating benefits, resources and burdens equally among the members, and if it gives equal protection to all. It is just if it allows horizontal and vertical mobility, if equal opportunity is the rule for all. This rule will prohibit discrimination on the grounds of race, colour, sex, and religion; for these would be irrelevant where they tend to lessen the human dignity and freedom of others. It is significant to note here that "equal opportunity" as a principle of social justice is interpreted according to proportionality of ability. Not everybody will have the same training and the same jobs. But the "sameness" of the principle of equality in the sense that one man's well-being is as valuable to him as any other's to himself or herself is to be maintained. The ideal is that each should receive according to his or her worth as human being, and according to merit, need and work. Equal opportunity does not mean drab monotony of qualitative identity.

Social injustice arises when the principle of equal opportunity is not observed, where there is discrimination between classes and groups with little or no social mobility, where the natural resources which nature provides for the benefit of all is placed in the hands of a few who exploit the labour of the rest or a great majority of the population who live on the level of paupers or almost so. In this respect, the balance of social justice should tend to level off the extremes, and provide each member with basic quality of life in terms of the available resources. Socially democratic arrangements tend to achieve this purpose.

Political justice concerns the ruling of political authority. Political authority derives ultimately from the social nature of man, from the fact that those conditions which make for the protection and full development of the individual as a social being cannot be achieved without authority being vested somehow in the community. Political authority makes for the dispensation of justice among members of the community.

The community, here, is not a mere abstraction, but consists of concrete individuals who are born free and equal. Since freedom and self-government are essential qualities of the person, political authority which, to a great extent, consists of decision-making as to how best to achieve the common good for the good life of the members of the community derives from the consent of the governed. And since democracy which is the government of the people, by the people, for the people is a vehicle which allows for the individual's expression of his consent to be governed as a responsible, respectable, free human being, genuine humanism espouses democratic goals. Democracy is based on compromise in the sense that it offers a solution to the conflict of rights among the free and equal.

The common good is the limit of political authority. Political injustice arises when political authority ceases to provide the common good, and is turned to the advantage of a few or majority against a few or majority. It results when political authority is abused to subjugate others to slavery as in a bad government; to use the words of Rousseau, "where equality is but apparent and illusory, it serves only to keep the poor man confined within the limits of his poverty, and so maintain the rich in their usurpation;"[33] and some are denied their human and civil rights. Here, politics becomes a pejorative term, a matter of intrigues, force and violence. Because political authority has degenerated into an instrument of domination, some thinkers like Karl Marx have tended to abolish the state through which political authority functions. But *abusus non tollit usum.*

In the extreme form, political injustice takes the form of subjugation in slavery as we have indicated. It also takes on the form of colonialism where force and violence are used to "pacify" another group or race. Here the "Right of War" or the "Right of the Strongest" finds full expression. We may recall here the argument of Socrates against Thrasymachus. There is no justice in such a situation. As Rousseau has eloquently shown, "Might does not create Right."[34] since might which is in the physical sphere cannot be transformed into right which is in the moral domain. To yield to the strongest is an act of necessity. Consequently, as he rightly points out, "a man enslaved, or a People conquered in war is under no obligation to obey the point at which force ceases to be operative."[35]

Hence, the colonial system, which is based on the right of the strongest or conqueror is a state of continuous force and injustice, because there cannot be a compact (between the conqueror and conquered), since no one makes a compact in which he comes off worse. Here Fanon echoes Rousseau.[36]

The above discussion provides us with a framework to evaluate Fanon's revolutionary humanism with reference to his seeking for justice.

The thrust of Fanon's humanism is the effort to make it possible for Blacks or the colonized to obtain justice in the social and political arrangements composed by Blacks and Whites, or Blacks alone. He was dismayed at the discrimination against the Negroes in the form of depriving them of human and civil rights, of the opportunity of living a fulfilled human life; in other words, at the crushing burden of the slavery and injustice in the colonial system.

Fanon was committed to the achievement of national independence on the part of the colonized. Political independence is *sine qua non* of political injustice on the part of the colonized. According to him, socio-political structures must have to meet the demands of justice and relevance for legitimation. He remarks:

> The function of a social structure is to set up institutions to serve man's needs. A society that drives its members to desperate solutions is a non-viable society, a society to be replaced.[37]
> . . .
> The worker in the commonwealth must cooperate in the social scheme of things. But he must be convinced of the excellence of the society in which he lives.[38]

We shall consider this in the next chapter in view of the alienation of the colonized.

Algeria was a case of foreign conquest and domination. Hence, according to the principle of political justice, "French Algeria" is a misnomer. The justification of the Algerian rebellion is based on this principle. And Fanon's revolutionary humanism derives much of its vigour from this fact.

To comment, with love and peace, the way of justice forms the harmony of fruitful human relationship. It is often said that where there is love there is no need for justice. Yet love contains an element of justice, in the sense that the lover respects the rights of the beloved and protects them. The union of the lover and the beloved is not a subsumption of the latter into the former. Hence, in intimacy the two retain at least their fundamental human rights, although in some situations, one can give up one's right for the good of the other. However, where there is love, justice becomes less perceptible because of the harmony which love brings in its train. Where there is no love, justice prepares the ground for love, and peace. The balance of peace derives from the balance of justice.

Aristotle's apt remark on the harmony of justice and friendship (love) at the political level is in place here:

> Friendship seems to hold states together, and lawgivers too care more for it than justice; for unanimity seems to be something like friendship, and this they aim at most of all, and expel faction as their worst enemy; and when men are friends

they have no need of justice, while when they are just they need friendship as well, and the truest form of justice is thought to be a friendly quality.[39]

Because of the apparent conflict, or rather the dialectic between man's tendency to self-interest and his altruistic tendency, between his good nature and aggressiveness, I think, the pursuit of justice, love and peace is a kind of conquest. This problem of conquest is at the centre of Fanon's revolutionary humanism.

Fanon wants to discover and love man wherever he may be."[40] He holds that human "consciousness is a process of transcendence to be haunted by the problem of love and understanding."[41] Peace comes from the *Yes* of man to man "which vibrates to cosmic harmonies."[42] Since the injustice and alienation of the colonial system are the main obstacles to love and peace, Fanon worked for the destruction of the colonial system as the crucial step toward peace and love. We shall see whether his espousal of revolutionary violence and decolonization constitutes an element of inconsistency in his humanism. Let us now consider the next important feature of his humanism, namely, its universalist scope.

4. UNIVERSALIST CHARACTER

Fanon expresses the universalist character of his humanism concretely as follows:

> In the absolute, the black is no more to be loved than the Czech, and truly what is to be done is to set man free.[43]

According to Fanon, the concern for the colonized reaches out to a universal concern for the wretched of the earth. He writes:

> I am a man, and what I have to recapture is the whole of the past world. I am not responsible solely for the revolt in San Domingo. Every time a man has contributed to the victory of the dignity of the spirit, every time a man has said no to an attempt to subjugate his fellows, I have felt solidarity with his act.[44]

Again:

> It is essential that the oppressed join up with the peoples who are already sovereign if a humanism that can be considered valid is to be built to the dimension of the universe.[45]

The process of liberation of man, independently of the concrete situations in which he finds himself, includes and concerns the whole of humanity. The fight for national dignity gives its true meaning to the struggle for bread and social dignity. This internal relation is one of the roots of the immense solidarity that unites the oppressed peoples to the exploited masses of the colonialist countries.[46]

With a tone reminiscent of Hegel's conception of history, he continues the note of universality:

The future of every man today has a relation of close dependence on the rest of the universe. That is why the colonial peoples must redouble their vigilance and their vigor. A new humanism can be achieved only at this price. The wolves must no longer find isolated lambs to prey upon. Imperialism must be blocked in all its attempts to strengthen itself. The peoples demand this; the historical process requires it.[47]

These passages show that Fanon envisages a new humanism in which Whites, Blacks and all peoples of colour will receive mutual recognition, and unite in fighting the common enemy of mankind, namely, colonial imperialism and all kinds of exploitation and oppression. It is the universalist's ethical thrust that gives glow to his humanism. This will be its strength and perhaps the source of its failure when we shall size up its consistency with regard to the use of violence.

This is all the more provocative, as we may remark here, in that a genuine humanist is committed to loving and caring for every man, to the intrinsic value of every man, even of his enemy; thus, he has the scope of a universalist ethics that transcends class or party. It is difficult to see how this can obtain in a revolutionary situation. This, I think, is the point of what I would call Fanon's dilemma.

We may add here that the problem with so many humanists who turn revolutionary is that they are class-conscious and regard the other as an enemy to be overthrown at any cost in the effort to establish their idology, even if on a transitional basis. To them, what is "good" is what furthers the ends of their class, and what is "evil" is what opposes it.[48] Violence, revolutionary violence is justified by them on the ground that it promotes the ideals of their particular class. They easily act on the principle that "the end justifies the means." We can see that a revolutionary humanist of this brand can easily become a contradiction of terms in advocating violence on the other.

He lacks the orientation to an authentically universal humanism. It appears that Fanon is not of this type. We shall see whether our investigation will prove the contrary in view of his espousal of revolutionary violence in the effort to ameliorate the social and political condition of the colonized and the oppressed. We now come to what may be called the climax of Fanon's humanism, that is, his conception of the emergence of a new man.

5. THE EMERGENCE OF A NEW MAN

At the end of his last book, *The Wretched of the Earth*, Fanon projects the emergence of a new man against the background of the inhumanity of the past:

> For Europe, for ourselves, and for humanity, comrades, we must turn a new leaf, we must work out new concepts, and *try to set afoot a new man.*[49]

To comment, the emergence of a new man requires a change of attitudes and the universalization of human values. It challenges the human creativity in all of us to transcend the contradictions involved in the social and political conflicts. The "new man" is a symbol of reconciliation.

The concept of a new man has an interesting history. The thrust of the Christian dispensation is the creation of a new man in all of us through the redemptive grace of Christ.[50] The "glow" of Karl Marx's philosophy derives, to a great extent, from his vision of the redemption of humanity through the proleterian revolution, and from it the creation of the new man as opposed to the old man who is alienated through the capitalist exploitation. Fanon's vision of the creation of a new man shares in this powerfully messianic vision. It is to his credit that the racial problem between the White and Black is portrayed in the context of an authentically universal humanism in which they are disalienated, complement one another, and not antagonize one another.

As the first step towards the creation of the new man, Fanon describes the alienated Black and White consciousness in what he calls a "clinical study," in *The Black Skin, White Masks*. We shall consider this in greater detail in the next chapter. Disalienation will result in the self-acceptance and affirmation of the Black vis-a-vis the White, his counterpart, in their mutual understanding and recognition of their humanity, and the common project of making an authentically universal humanism work. Fanon insists on the recognition of the Black man. The Black man has the right to live and contribute towards the civilization of mankind.

However, antagonistic forces stand on the way of which the most vehement is colonial exploitation and racism. The creation of the new man will therefore entail the overthrow of the colonial system which dehumanizes. Violence constitutes a radical element in the process of bringing the new man to birth. We shall see in the fifth chapter the solution of the problem or dilemma involved in this conception of the new man.

6. DIALECTICAL CHARACTER

Another important feature of Fanon's humanism is its dialectical underpinning. Fanon derives his conception of dialectic from Hegel and Marx with whom the concept is often associated today, even though the term "dialectic" has taken on various meanings since Plato. Hence, in order to appreciate the dialectical features of Fanon's humanism it is necessary to know the conception of "dialectic" in Hegel and Marx.

In Hegel dialectic is a movement in which there is essentially an internal negation or contradiction in thought itself. The negative is the moving principle of the self-development of a concept or reality. Essential to dialectic is the "comprehension of the unity of opposites or of the positive in the negative."[51] Every negation is a kind of determination: The clarity of concepts is inherently linked with the opposite. In a more complex form, the dialectic consists of a movement in which there is first the thesis (affirmation, position) which provokes the antithesis (negation, contradiction), and then the synthesis (resolution) in which the former two stages are transcended. Contradiction and the overcoming of it at the higher level of synthesis are essential to the Hegelian dialectic. According to Hegel, dialectic, as the principle of all movements, pervades reality. In his book, *The Phenomenology of Spirit,* he describes the movement of consciousness in self-realization as a dialectical movement in which each mode of consciousness in realizing itself in a higher form is negated. In the political sphere a classical example of a dialectical movement is the case of an authoritarian regime (thesis) provoking the rise of a revolutionary regime (antithesis), which eventually becomes a moderate form of democracy (synthesis).

We have seen how Hegel presents the interaction of the master and slave as a dialectic. Here, the contradictions involved require resolution because the master and slave relationship is not truly human relationship. Hence, the reciprocal interaction of the two consciousnesses leads to the recognition of their mutual dependence. For all his alleged power, superiority and independence, the master comes to realize that he depends on the slave. A higher form of relation which is truly human is called for. Hegel perceptively points up that self-consciousness is what it is by a mutual recognition of another self-consciousness. It is free when it recognizes another self-consciousness as free. Consequently, a society that practises slavery is not truly free.[52] Hegel also describes the historical process as the dialectical movement of the Spirit.

Marx adopts Hegel's dialectic as a dialectic of negativity, but he converts the abstract movement of the Absolute Spirit into a movement of human praxis; that is, Marx translates Hegel's concern for the Absolute Spirit into that of man's relation with nature and to each other.

Fanon draws directly from Hegel as we have seen in his quotation and comment on Hegel's dialectic of the Master and the Slave, and also from Marx's adoption. Fanon agrees with Marx on the point that human praxis is a process in which the dialectic is important, but Fanon stresses the socio-political and cultural milieu. But unlike Marx who believes in the inevitable and objective dialectic of material forces in the historical process without the freedom of man shaping events, Fanon maintains the transcendence and freedom of man in the dialectic of man with the environment and with each other in the historical process. Man is free and therefore, is responsible for the creation of socio-political order at the present and in the future. "The hand of history is the hand of man."[53]

To Fanon each person is responsible for shaping his destiny and is not entirely at the mercy of blind forces:

> The body of history does not determine a single of my actions. I am my own foundation. And it is my going beyond the historical instrumental hypothesis that I will initiate the cycle of my freedom.[54]

Consequently, he stresses the human intervention in the dialectics of the historical process of decolonization on the part of the colonized. Decolonization or liberation is not the "fruit of an objective dialectic which more or less rapidly assumes the appearance of an absolutely inevitable mechanism."[55] It is up to the colonized or oppressed to initiate the stage of negation (antithesis) in the dialectics of revolution. He writes:

Africa shall be free. Yes, but it must get to work, it must not lose sight of its own unity . . .

Africa will not be free through the mechanical development of material forces, but it is the hand of the African and his brain that will set into motion and implement the dialectics of the liberation of the continent . . . the Africans must remember that there is not an objective optimism that is more or less mechanically inevitable, but that optimism must be the sentiment that accompanies the revolutionary commitment and the combat.[56]

Although the process of the liberation of the colonial peoples is inevitable according to the historical process, the national liberation is the work of the oppressed people. They have to take their destiny in their own hand.

It is to Fanon's credit that he sees the racial and colonial problem as a dialectical process.[57] He describes it in the chapter on racism and culture. According to him, racism is a dimension of the colonial system; that is, "of the systematic oppression of a people."[58]

Historically speaking, colonialism arose from military confrontation of peoples, races, and groups. Then began the economic exploitation of the native population for the enrichment of the "mother" country. The domination of oppression is legitimated by "scientific arguments" which allegedly show up the oppressed group or race to be inferior. The alienation of the native may take the form of assimilation, the loss of cultural identity or its disruption, through which the social group imitate the oppressor. On this Fanon writes:

The oppressor, through the inclusive and frightening character of his authority, manages to impose on the native new ways of seeing, and in particular, a pejorative judgment with respect to his original forms of existing.[59]

All this constitutes the thesis stage.

However, this alienation is never wholly successful. The oppressed people begin to assert themselves by challenging the injustice of their condition, of being deculturized by devaluing their cultural system and accepting the culture of the colonial master. They begin to dig into their past. Thus, the second stage (antithesis) of the dialectics of racism and culture begins. On this point Fanon writes:

Discovering the futility of alienation, his progressive deprivation, the inferiorized individual, after this phase of deculturation, of estraneousness, comes back to his original position.

* * *

He embraces his forgotten culture with passion . . . the oppressed goes into ecstasies over every discovery. The wonder
is permanent. Having formerly emigrated from his culture, the
native today explores it with ardor. It is a continual honey-
moon. Formerly inferiorized, he is now in a state of grace.[60]

Fanon points out that the enslaved people in swinging back
to their dying culture which is only held up by traditionalists,
discover that their rediscovered institutions no longer corres-
pond to the complexity of technical development. The problem
is how to reconcile the traditional values with technical development. This will take time and insight. However, as Fanon
points out, the good effect of discovering their culture is the
emergence of a new attitude which no longer ridicules their
tradition. This means that the group no longer runs away from
itself, since "the sense of the past is rediscovered" and identified with the truth; that is, to use the words of Heidegger, the
natives discover their being-in-the-world. Through this redeeming discovery which initiates the crucial stage of self-affirmation, the oppressed people, according to Fanon, now espouses
the cause of liberation "with full knowledge of what is involved
in fighting all forms of exploitation and alienation of man."[61]

On the other hand, the oppressor appeals to assimilation to
integration, to community. But, for the native, the discovery
of the past is the condition and source of freedom; and this
makes it possible for him to be galvanized into action with the
whole fibre of his being. The myth of his inferiority collapses
because, in the struggle the colonized assert his equality with
the colonizer.

At this stage, Fanon continues, the racist group points ac-
cusingly to manifestation of racism among the oppressed. However, here, the third stage of the dialectics emerges in which
the two cultures are transcended by the universality which "re-
sides in this decision to recognize and accept the reciprocal
relativism of different cultures, once the colonial status is
irreversibly excluded."[62] This is the final stage of Fanon's revolutionary humanism which attempts to resolve the contradictions of the colonial or oppressive system. The affirmation
of the colonial power with its train of injustice and discrimination, the seed of contradiction, has provoked opposition, on the
part of the colonized who assert themselves by counter force.
Their dialectics eventuate in the overcoming of the original

position of each side, and in the recognition of each other. With the destruction or withering away of colonialism, this stage shows up the right of peoples to self-determination with its enriching relationship among free peoples. In the following chapter we shall consider in detail the crisis situation, the alienation of the colonized which calls for resolution in order to preserve human values.

Chapter III

THE CRISIS SITUATION: ALIENATION OF THE COLONIZED

The preceding chapter has thrown light on the features of Fanon's humanism, especially on those values which constitute the fabric of a human world. However, the question remains as to Fanon's description of the situation which represents the negation of those values. When humanistic values are absent through deprivation or opposed by antagonistic forces, a crisis situation or alienating condition develops. Fanon's revolutionary humanism is a reaction to the condition of alienation of the colonized or oppressed.

Man's self-realization is a dialectical process with the environment. From the point of view of revolutionary humanism, the environment is socio-political. Fanon emphasizes the importance of the social environment in the development and alienation of the individual and group.[1] As we have indicated, he maintains that the individual or worker in the society ought to cooperate in the social and political arrangements for personal development, and be convinced of their relevance and excellence or of the possibility of improving them.[2] Where the possibility of improvement is blocked, alienation which precipitates into a crisis arises. In this chapter we shall consider this crisis situation with particular reference to the alienating condition of the colonial system about which Fanon was chiefly concerned.

In describing the alienation of the colonized or oppressed, Fanon was influenced by Hegel, Marx, Sartre, Freud, Adler and others. Consequently a philosophical reflection on his description of the alienation of the colonized may include a reflection on the psychological and psychoanalytical elements.

1. MEANING OF ALIENATION

The term "alienation" is a key concept in most of the human sciences. Since it takes on various meanings, it needs a brief explanation. It derives from the Latin verb "alienare" which literally means "to make something another's, to take away." In the legal sphere it refers to the transfer of title to property. Used with reference to states of consciousness, it indicates a frame of mind in which a person loses his or her reason or senses, is estranged, does not feel at home with himself or herself, and feels some discordance.

Today the term has a wide range of use: it refers to "an extraordinary variety of psycho-social disorders, including loss of self, anxiety states, anomie, despair, depersonalization, rootlessness, apathy, social disorganization, loneliness, atomization, powerlessness, meaninglessness, isolation, pessimism, and the loss of beliefs or values."[3] As we shall see, Fanon's use of the term or its equivalent includes some of the above.

Since his conception of alienation derives, to some extent from Hegel and Marx, whose names come to mind when alienation is mentioned in the philosophical context, and furthermore, since their analysis constitutes a critical framework for Fanon's analysis, it is appropriate to discuss them briefly in order to see how Fanon adapts their use of the term.

2. ALIENATION IN HEGEL AND MARX

In his philosophy, Hegel uses the term "alienation" with reference to the Spirit (Phenomenology of Mind) and to right (Philosophy of Right). In its literal sense, as we have seen, the corresponding German word is Entfremdung which is derived from entfremden (to make another's). In the Philosophy of Right the term used to stand for alienation is "verausserung" (conveyance of the title of property to another).

At the level of the Spirit, alienation refers to the state of consciousness which has become aware of "otherness" or "separation" of something, or a disharmony between the individual and the social substance (Bildung, culture) which Hegel regards as the universal aspect of man, or between the actual condition of an individual and his essential nature (self-alienation). In another sense, alienation denotes a surrender or sacrifice which is made of particularity and willfulness in favour of unity which is universal.[4]

According to Hegel, the Spirit is "consciously aware of itself as its own world and of the world as itself."[5] Since the Spirit is free, it can exteriorize itself through creation (culture, social substance); that is, it can abandon its actual (present) structure in order to acquire a new and more complex one. The two are, however, in a dialectical opposition to each other. It can create a transcendent world of faith which is opposed to the actual world. When this happens and it is preoccupied with the transcendent world of faith without recognizing its content in the actual present, it becomes alienated. Hegel expresses the two levels of alienation of the Spirit, thus:

> The one is the actual world, that of self-estrangement, the other is that which Spirit constructs for itself in the ether of pure consciousness, raising itself above the first. This second world, being constructed in opposition and contrast to that estrangement, is just on that account not free from it; on the contrary, it is only the other form of that estrangement, which consists precisely in having a conscious existence in two sorts of words, and embraces both.[6]

The aim of Hegel in his phenomenological analysis of the movement of consciousness or Spirit is to show that the particular is a dialectical aspect of the unity of the Universal which he calls the Absolute. His analysis describes a concrete universal or the abstract universal becoming concrete. Hence the Spirit is alienated or "self-estranged" when it does not recognize itself as universal. In order to become universal, the complete independence of the individual or particular structure must be transcended or surrendered in the dialectical synthesis for the unity of the universality. Here this surrender or sacrifice which is made for realizing the unity of the universality, as we have seen, is denoted by Hegel as alienation.

From the socio-political point of view, Hegel locates alienation in the opposition of consciousness to the power and wealth of the State, and also in the opposition of an individual's consciousness to the social substance (culture). What he calls the base consciousness is alienated because "it looks upon the authoritative power of the State as a chain, as something suppressing its separate existence for its own sake, and hence hates the ruler, obeys only with secret malice, and stands ever ready to burst out in rebellion. It sees, too, in wealth, by which it attains to the enjoyment of its own independent existence, merely something discordant."[7] According to Hegel, the base consciousness is revolutionary consciousness because it questions the absolute power and wealth of the State. This criticism of the base consciousness is premised on Hegel's idea that the

State has absolute power and should dominate the individual in order to have objective freedom. It may be said, I think, that the base consciousness is asserting or implying that the State is meant to serve the common good concretized in the good of individual members of society, and therefore agitates for reform or resolution. Hegel sees it triumphing in the French Revolution. Yet, much as he disapproves of the terrors of the French Revolution, he cannot but approve of its ideals of equality, freedom and fraternity. However, he considers it as a moment in the dialectic of history, and the absolute power of the State is never questioned. On the contrary, what he calls noble consciousness gives unquestioning obedience to the absolute power of the State in which "it feels its own essential nature to exist, is conscious of its own purpose and absolute content."[8] Hegel has high regard for this kind of consciousness because of its virtue which consists in "heroism of service," that is, acting in self-abandonment for the sake of the prevailing power. However, it is worth remarking that Hegel's analysis of this cast of mind may lead to totalitarian outlook.

The question, one may ask, is what should happen when the State *de facto* no longer serves as the universal aspect of man, and is used by the powers-that-be for their corrupt ends, for oppressing the masses. The pertinence of this question can be seen when one considers the position of Hegel in his early political essay on the political situation in Wurttenberg(1798). Here he agitates for reform and takes to task those who wanted to hold on to political institutions "which no longer agree with the customs, the needs, the opinions of mankind and from which the Spirit has fled." Apparently, this move in agitating for reform contradicts his criticism of the base consciousness for agitating for reform or revolution. It is also contrary to his position when he wrote the introduction to his essay on the German constitution in 1802. Here he describes the existing order in order to exhort the people to accept it even though he saw that it needed a lot of improvement. He writes:

> The thoughts contained in this work can serve no purpose or effect . . . other than that of the comprehending of what exists, and thus of the promotion of a more tranquil attitude toward it, together with a moderate toleration of it in word and deed. For it is not what exists that makes us vehement and causes us suffering; rather, it is what is not as it should be. But if we see that it is as it must be—i.e., that it is not contrary or accidental— then we also see that it should be as it is. (13, 5).[9]

This passage accords with Hegel's dictum, "The real (actual) is rational." In view of this, Richard Schacht holds that the above passage should be interpreted in the light of Hegel's belief in gradual evolution or improvement of existing institutions. Consequently, to remove the logical difficulties involved in Hegel's own formulation of the sense of "necessary" and "must be" Schacht distinguishes two senses of necessary: the strong sense ("could not be otherwise") and the weak sense ("not arbitrary"). Thus he reformulates Hegel's position:

> One may believe that existing institutions are far from perfect, but that real, lasting improvement of them can come about only through gradual historical evolution. Indeed, one may believe that agitation for change not only is unlikely to result in the acceleration of this evolution, but rather moreover is highly likely to have precisely the opposite effect, and to result in a change for the worse. If these assumptions are valid, it would follow that things are as they "should be," in the sense that the world could not be better than it is at this time. Hegel made something like these assumptions, and drew these conclusions."[10]

But, on the other hand, as Schacht rightly points out, these assumptions are less compelling, when one sees counterexamples in the political and social history of the last century and half, in which radical action (revolution) did not miscarry. Therefore, comprehension and resignation, as means of overcoming alienation, at best, are only plausible. The attitude of just comprehending the actual and being resigned to it seem to play down the force of Hegelian dialectic in which opposition is essential, and is overcome on a higher level of synthesis. It may be said that at this period in his career, Hegel vacillated as he donned the garb of the philosopher of the Prussian State.

The question of the abuse of the power and wealth of the State constitutes the crux of Karl Marx's critique of Hegel's philosophy of the State in the *Philosophy of Right*. Marx agrees with Feuerbach's criticism of Hegel's concept of philosophy, "that philosophy is nothing more than religion brought into thought and developed by thought, and that it is to be equally to be condemned as another form and mode of existence of human alienation," because he thought that it did not refer to the problems and solutions of the human, socio-political life just as religion does.[11] In this criticism of religion, Feuerbach claims that religion constitutes the alienation of man, that God is nothing but the expression of the potentialities of man projected into the beyond.[12] To overcome alienation, man must recognize himself as God. Thus, Feuerbach reduces religion to anthropology. He criticizes Hegel's dialectical relation as abstract, and reduces it to the social relation of man to man in concrete material life. Marx points out in the *Critique of Hegel's Dialectic* that "Hegel has merely discovered an *abstract, logical,* and speculative expression of the historical process, which has not yet the real history of man as a given subject, but only the history of the *act of creation,* of the *genesis of man.*"[13] According to him what is needed is a real history of man in human praxis. Thus, in his criticism of Hegel's philosophy of the State which Hegel regards as the expression of the Spirit, Marx criticizes him for locating alienation on the level of the spirit rather than bringing it down to the specific problems of the socio-political life.

In contrast to Hegel's view that the State is the expression of the Spirit, Marx sees the State as an instrument of perpetuating the right of primogeniture whereby private property is acquired by the princes and nobles without the responsibility of ameliorating the social conditions. Hence, on Marx's showing, the State is an instrument of oppression, because the propertied class use private property legitimated by the State to control the working class; for the worker eeks out existence, and does not enjoy the fruit of his labor which the capitalists, the propertied class enjoy; thus the worker is alienated.

The thrust of Marx's argument is to explain alienation in socio-economic terms. At different periods of his writing he locates it in different economic factors: first in man's estrangement from his productive activity in which he should find self-fulfillment *(Economic Manuscripts),* then in division of labour where the worker competes against his fellow men who become pawns and means for his personal aggrandizement *(German Ideology),* in money *(The Capital),* and in the formation of class, the very notion of which implies destitution and struggle *(Communist Manifesto).* Alienation culminates in the dialectical polarization of the classes (bourgeoisie and proletariat), which leads to the proletarian revolution in which private property is abolished and, via the temporary dictatorship of the proletariat, the State withers away, and a classless society is established. In the proletarian revolution the masses are redeemed, and in them, all mankind. Revolution is an essential means of ending the alienation of man. The classless society will give birth to a new man.

3. FANON ON THE ALIENATION
OF THE NEGRO, THE COLONIZED

Fanon describes the alienation of the Negro, the colonized with characteristic candour. Just as Marx sees alienation in terms of socio-economic factors, Fanon sees the alienation of the Negro, the colonized, as essentially socio-economic, but it is a socio-economic alienation that has profound psychological effects. But his exploration of the alienation and disalienation of the Black man bears the stamp of Hegel's influence.

It may be more correct to say that he treats of the alienation of Blacks at two levels: at the intellectual level of self and cultural identity and affirmation, and at the socio-economic level which has psychological effects. Both levels are intertwined in his treatment so that it is difficult to separate them. He speaks about the alienation of the Negro in terms of cultural imposition, and of the exploitation of the native by the colonists, just as Marx sees the alienations of the proletariat as their exploitation by the bourgeoisie.

Fanon maintains that the inferiority complex of the Negro is the result of interiorizing economic insecurity and oppression and not a biological strain. He defines colonization as the systematic conquest of a national territory, in which oppression is perpetuated by force and violence:

> The Negro problem does not resolve itself into the problem of living among white man but rather of Negroes exploited, enslaved, despised by colonialists, capitalist society that is only accidentally white.[14]

According to Fanon, the world is divided according to race and levels of economic development. The economic structure in the colonies becomes the instrument of domination or oppression of the racist colonial system: "You are rich because you are white; you are white because you are rich."[15] And "one is white above a certain financial level."[16] One can easily understand Fanon's interpretation of alienation in the form of racism in economic terms if one takes into account his fundamental humanistic presupposition that all men are equal, and his rejection of biological interpretation of racism. The Negro, he asserts, is "not a creature of biology but of oppression." He argues that it is impossible to enslave men without making them inferiors. This is especially true where there is a difference of color between the colonists and the colonized. Thus, he contends that colonialism inevitably gives rise to racism.

Fanon holds that by various tactics the colonial power or the oppressor keeps down the oppressed: Certain myths are conjured up to prevent the moment of awareness. In the context of racism, these myths are meant to show up the inferiority of the oppressed race.[17] For example, the theory of the absence of cortical integration, the comparative form of the skull of the colonial people, the "emotional instability of the Negro," and the low I.Q. ratings are examples of myths that solidify prejudice and oppression. Fanon rejects these "scientific arguments."[18] He strongly criticizes M. Mannoni, who in his book, *Prospero and Caliban: Psychology of Colonization*, struck up the theory of the dependence complex of the colonial people of Malagasy.[19]

On the human level these arguments have been used, for the worse, with the logical consequence of portraying the Negro as sub-human. Zoologically described by the White counterpart, he is regarded as a beast, as an incarnation of sexual potency, and of lust.[20] These poignant myths made it impossible for the Negro to live in and for himself. He was always confronted with the stereotyped image which these myths make of him. Since he was overdetermined from the outside by these myths, it was almost an impossible task to liberate himself. In an attempt to escape from them, he has not made the first crucial move to recognize and accept himself. In the absence of self-affirmation, the Negro wanted to be White, to embrace White culture in order to have his humanity recognized.

(i) Alienation as Cultural Imposition: Language

One of the major aspects of alienation is cultural imposition in the form of language. The importance of this aspect may be gauged from the fact that Fanon devotes a chapter to its exposition.[21] By way of commentary, language incarnates and expresses the culture of a people. Since it is a distinctively human quality, the deprivation of language amounts to a deprivation of a person's humanity. It is a great power in man for objectivating himself. Incorrect or fumbling use of language leads to confusion and even to unintelligibility, and so to lack of sociality. We often feel the power of words when they issue from the mouth of great speakers. Language is not only the standard of judging a person or culture, but also a means of assuming a culture, and of supporting a civilization.[22]

Fanon, therefore, confronts the problem of the Negroes of the Antilles and of the colonized who are alienated because of the fact of language. As the French language was regarded as the language of civilization, the Antillean Negro considered himself White or human to the extent that he mastered the French Language. He regarded the Creole as a symbol of inferiority, and lack of civilization. Hence the Antillean wanted to get away from it, and his dream was to embrace the French of Paris. Unfortunately for him, the road from Martinique to Paris was difficult, in the sense that, on his arrival at Paris, his accent betrayed him; he found himself discriminated against on this ground. However, some who succeeded in polishing themselves with good French return home with airs and graces, and would not like to be identified with the less fortunate. We may call this a form of intellectual alienation. We may add here that the situation is different where bilingualism is recognized. Here a second language is an asset and may not be regarded as a form of alienation.

(ii) Colour Prejudice

Another important level of the Negro's alienation is that he is a victim of colour prejudice. According to Fanon, the fact of being black created a ghost of fear in the Black man in the presence of the White man, because it was viewed as a symbol of the bad character, and evil. Fanon devotes two chapters to this problem,[23] and describes the agonizing experiences of Black women who tried to ape the White woman, wanted to marry White men in the effort to escape from "the dark night of blackness;"[24] and also the experiences of Black men who wanted to embrace the White civilization by marrying White women, and thus acquire recognition.[25] Fanon describes Mayotte Capecia as an example and symbol of the first. From childhood she had dreamed of marrying a White man, but unfortunately she is deluded into a relationship with Andre, a White man, in which authentic love could not be born because of colour prejudice. As she wrote in her book, *Je Suis Martinique,* Fanon recalls:

> I should have liked to be married, but to a white man. But a woman of color is never altogether respected in a white man's eyes. Even if when he loves her. I knew that.[26]

Being a victim of unconscious conflicts of colour prejudice Fanon points out, she cannot enjoy authentic love which "unites the permanent values of human reality—entails the mobilization of psychic drives basically freed of unconscious conflicts."[27] Fanon contends that her dreams make her a good case "of

Hegel's subjective certainty made flesh."[28] Many a Negress of Mayotte's calibre has become neurotic. Jean Veneuse, a Negro born in the Antilles, but who had become "European" by living in Bordeaux, is an example and symbol of the Negro encountering frustration in attempting to marry or cultivate intimate relationships with a White woman in order to attain recognition. Fanon analyzes these imperfections and perversions of love to clear the ground for understanding genuine love.

Fanon, furthermore, maintains that the Antillean Negro lived an ambiguous life which makes him extraordinarily neurotic. From the psychological point of view, he points out that the Martinicans, both Black and White are victims of what he calls a "European collective unconcious," that is, unreflecting social prejudice, another expression for those myths which we have already considered, that turned the Black man into a symbol of evil, his colour into bad projections, and thought of him in terms of sexual potency rather than rationality. Early on, Fanon finds himself guilty of it:

I am a white man. For unconsciously I distrusted what is black in me, that is, the whole of my being.[29]

This "collective unconscious" is a psychological projection of what the White man hates in himself. The Black man becomes the scapegoat of the White man. Fanon claims that just as it is the anti-Semite who creates the Jew (distorted image of the Jew),[30] so it is the Negrophobe who creates the Negro. The Negro and the Jew are companions of the misery of being the scapegoat. In order to react against anti-Semitism, the Jew turns himself into an anti-Semite.[31] The same can be said of the Negro who is always fighting his own image because "his moral consciousness implies a kind of scission, a fracture of consciousness into a bright part and an opposing black part. In order to achieve morality it is essential that the black, the dark, the Negro vanish from consciousness."[32] But care must be taken to avoid the error of assimilating anti-Semitism to Negrophobia.

Fanon observes that the Negro child in Antilles loses his or her normalcy in the first contact with the White culture, particularly with its "collective unconscious" which he or she absorbes from comic books, newspapers, textbooks, advertisements, films and radio. Even by 1940, before Aime Cesaire arrived, Antilleans would never dream of being called Negroes. Fanon further observes that when the Negro makes contact with the White world, he may be so sensitized that his ego collapses if his psychic structure is not strong. He no longer behaves like "an *actional* person." The goal of his behaviour would be the other (in the guise of the White man) who gives him worth. In Adlerian terminology, he would live by comparison with the other (White man) who reflects what he wants to see, his superiority in order to gain security. However, unlike Alfred Adler who locates the comparison neurosis on the personal level, Fanon locates it in the social environment. Fanon recounts some of his personal experiences of colour prejudice which grips the reader's attention.

In dealing with the problem of alienation, Fanon makes the point that both Whites and Blacks are alienated. In his description of the relationship of the Black and White, he points up that the Black consciousness (Black people's individual and social consciousness) fails to recognize itself, and has taken flight in the mirage of trying to be White. The Negro consciousness is sealed in its inferiority complex. The White consciousness, on the other hand, is sealed in its superiority complex with fear of equality with the Negro. It has failed to recognize the fact that the recognition of its humanity also depends on the recognition of the humanity of the Black consciousness. Furthermore, the Black consciousness (Black man) has failed to recognize that the blackness of its skin is an aspect of its self-identity.[33] Fanon considers the sealing of the Black man with myths of inferiority, with its consequent injustices by the White man in terms of Jasper's concept of metaphysical guilt against humanity.

(iii) The Colonial System

The alienation or opposition of the two consciousnesses reaches a climax in the deprivation and exploitation of the colonial system. Because of the deprivation of human values and the rampant violence in maintaining the colonial system, Fanon describes it as a Manichean world. It is a divided world, that of the native and of the colonizer, that of darkness and light, of vice and virtue. It is a world in which the native is regarded by the colonizer and oppressor as a symbol of evil, as "insensitive to ethics . . . the negation of values."[34] It is a world in which "the settler never ceases to be an enemy, the opponent, the foe that must be overthrown."[35] It is a world of opposition between the well-fed and the hungry, the rich and the destitute, the haves and the have-nots. Fanon echoes Marx who described the dialectics of opposition in the industrial society as a class struggle between the bourgeoisie (capitalists) and the proletariat (the workers). Thus, he divides the world into two classes: the natives, the colonized, the poor, on the one hand, and the rich colonialists on the other.

The collapse of the derogatory myths about the Negro is inevitable in the dialectics of revolutionary humanism. It opens the way for the oppressed to discover their own minds. Because the colonial power negates the values of the other person and denies him all human qualities, Fanon argues that it forces the people it dominates to ask themselves the soul-searching question: "In reality, who am I?" This question reaches down to the smouldering consciousness and the sense of human dignity, justice and love in the oppressed, and eventuates in the discovery of the Negro mind. Since there are two levels of alienation, according to Fanon, arising from the intellectual and the exploitative,[36] the liberation of Black consciousness is staged at the socio-political and psychological levels. In order to show the need for decolonization we may now discuss the seeds of contradiction in the colonial system with reference to its ethics as a critical framework.

4. Ethics of Colonial Imperialism

Colonial imperialism is the subjugation of a people for economic gains. Historically speaking, colonial imperialism arose from military confrontation of peoples, races and groups. The military campaigns of the French, the British, the Portuguese, the Italians and the Belgians against the natives of Africa,[37] India and America are cases in point. The result of the colonial wars in Africa was the partitioning of Africa by the Western powers by a stroke of the pen on the maps, the creation of artificial boundaries in which different ethnic groups were lumped together to make artificial units (colonies). The constants of colonial imperialism at the beginning are force and violence by which the natives are subjugated.[38] The operative principles here are "Might is right," and "Divide and rule." Violence is legitimized, and it continues to be the principle of action right through to the end.

The "law and order" set up is from the point of view of the colonizing power; and as a means of pacification, its violent nature in time becomes imperceptible through acceptance. In some cases the colonial system brings about a radical disorientation of the life and values of the native; and in some others, the natives are allowed to continue to maintain their native laws and customs insofar as they are not opposed to the ag-

grandisement of the colonial power. Since colonial imperialism is a venture of subjugation for economic gains, the recognition of the humanity of the colonized is at the lowest degree.
As M. Winslow pertinently expressed it: "Colonies not only
produced gold and silver, but in the broader sense they were
regarded as 'gold mines.'"[39] For example, "the colonies were
valuable means of redressing England's unfavorable balance
of trade in Europe." At the human level, the alienating condition of colonies was succinctly expressed by Postlethwayt as
follows:

> It is a law founded on the very nature of colonies that they
> ought to have no other culture or arts wherein to rival the arts
> and culture of the parent country.[40]

Colonial imperialism is allied to militarism. Those who
justify colonial imperialism on the ground of "civilizing mission" fail to appreciate the logic of its all-consuming passion
for economic gains. On this Winslow writes:

> And there is truth also in the simple conclusion which history
> has taught some of its chroniclers, that imperialism is a
> demonstration of the principle that the more you have, the
> more you have to hold what you have.[41]

"Civilized governments," Hobson says, "may undertake the
political and economic control of lower races . . . Such inter-
ference with the government of a lower race must be directed
primarily to secure the safety and progress of the civilization
of the world, and not the special interest of the interfering nation."[42] But his optimism was overweighed by the gloom of concrete facts. The mandate policy, at its best, is still vitiated by
racial prejudice which fails to recognize the deep-seated human
desire for recognition. It is a contradiction of terms to talk of
progress of civilization while holding on to racism, the doc-
trine that one race is inferior to another. This is the moot point
in the philosophy of decolonization. The strength of Fanon
lies in articulating this philosophy.

It is worthwhile to remark here that the common good as advocated by the colonial power and guaranteed by its laws is often
suspect. Often a double standard is used by the colonial power:
one for its citizens and one for the colony where the talk of humanity and human standards receives a slant by virtue of the
fact that the native, if he is of a different race, is discriminated
against as an inferior, or as a slave as the result of conquest.[43]
In the case where the colony is of a different race, racial pre-

47

judice is an added dimension of colonial imperialism. An attempt is made by the colonial power to justify colonial imperialism by saying that it is a means of bringing the colonized race into the light of civilization. Deculturation takes place by the devalorization of the native culture. The colonial system is arranged in such a way as to show the native the inferiority of his culture, and he is made to ape the colonist.

Where the native population is illiterate, the colonial power introduces education. The motive is not purely humanitarian; education is a means of getting some of the natives to operate the system. Hence, priority is placed on clerical training. In some areas, the colonial power puts a limit to the standard to be reached by those who are being educated so as not to equip them for managerial positions. The managerial positions are manned by expatriates from the mother country.

With regard to economic growth of the dependent people, there is little or no move on the part of the colonial power to establish industries in the colony. The colony is a place for the production of raw materials for feeding the industries of the mother country, and a market for her finished products.[44]

Where the climate is congenial there is a movement from the colonialist country to settle in the colonial territory. Hence, the problem of coexistence with the native population emerges. Where the colonialist is of the same race as the natives there is integration by marriage. But where they are of different races and colour there may be a move toward segregation[45] or occasionally, an integration by intermarriage.[46] In the former case there is a glaring inequality between the natives and the settlers with regard to economic growth. The settler is a man of wealth and power. He holds the native in contempt as inferior. The native is deprived of economic growth by systematic exploitation through slave labour and discrimination.[47]

This gloomy picture of the colonial world is not without its silver lining. The education which has been introduced by the colonial power becomes an instrument of liberation on the part of the colonized. Education in the colonial world produces an elite which stands astride of two worlds, that of the colonial power and that of the native culture. The members of the elitist group work for the improvement of the lot of their people. They demand improvement in education. They constitute the progressive front. Some of the elite work for a gradual, peaceful movement to independence, and some others become radicalized at the sight of the inhuman condition of their people, and spearhead of violent liberation movement.[48] In some cases colonial power adopts a centralist and assimilative policy in the colony.[49] In these cases some of the elite would only aspire to have themselves recognized in the assimilative culture of the colonial power. The radicalized group will galvanize against this. World opinion against colonialism often makes the colonial powers loosen the clutches of power. This may lead to a non-violent victory for independence for the colony. But where the colonial power resists, maintains power by force and violence, and insists on its "right" to rule, appeals to reason and negotiation are out of the question. The failure or impossibility of peaceful demonstration forces the natives into the dialectic of a war of liberation. As the colonial power insists on its "right" by force of arms, it is hard to see how the right of the natives to their own can be recognized and maintained without resort to force and violence. This is the lesson of history.

5. The Case of Algeria

Algeria exemplifies a case of colonial domination, and of the problems of the colonial system. The thrust of French colonizing policy dates back to June 14, 1830 when the French invaded Algiers. It is not accidental that this invasion took place when the regime of Charles X was becoming unpopular. As Edgar O'Balance has pointed out, the immediate aim of the invasion was not so much the desire for colonial aggrandisement as the desire to turn the mind of the French people from the increasing unpopularity of this government by a victory in style and scope as grand as Napoleon's.[50]

It has been said that the invasion was the result of an alleged insult of a French consul by the Dey of Algiers. The French government owed large sums of money to some French Algerian Jewish traders since the time of the Revolution. The Dey of Algiers intervened on behalf of his Jewish subjects, and summoned the French consul for an interview. It was alleged that the Dey grew impatient at the lack of progress in the interview, and struck the French consul with a fly whisk.[51]

Three years after this incident, French troops invaded Algiers, and, after three weeks of heavy fighting, took it by storm. Resistance in the countryside under the leadership of Emir Abd al Qadir was finally broken, and the countryside was pacified.

The pacification of Algeria took a heavy toll of lives and property. The ravages and atrocities were described by two French generals, Bugeand and St. Arnand:

More than 50 fine villages, built of stone and roofed with tiles, were destroyed. Our soldiers made very considerable pickings there. We did not have the time, in the heat of combat, to chop down the trees. The task, in any case, would have been beyond our strength. Twenty thousand men armed with axes could not in six months cut down the olives and fig trees which cover the beautiful landscape which lay at our feet.

There were still numerous bands of the enemy on the summits, and I was hoping for another engagement. But they refused to come down and I began to chop down the fine orchards and to set fire to the magnificent villages under the enemy's eyes. (1846)

I left in wake a vast conflagration. All the villages, some 200 in number, were burnt down, all the gardens destroyed, all the olive trees cut down. (1851)[52]

An era of colonization followed the French pacification of Algeria and its countryside. Fertile and rich lands were expropriated from the Muslim inhabitants and given to a horde of unemployed, exiled and political misfits from France for settlement. As the common French man was not attracted to emigrate to Algeria, it was the French policy to invite immigrants from Europe, especially those of Mediterranean origin. These settlers were called "colons." Their number reached 109,400 by 1874, with a minority of 47,000 of French origin.[53]

Algeria was eventually incorporated into the French hegemony as a department of Metropolitan France. Private companies were induced to settle by land offer. The colons developed large-scale agriculture which was subsidized from France. Among other products, cereals and wine were the most important. The productivity of the large-scale farms of the colons was a great contrast to the poor production of the Muslims' small farms in the rural areas. The colons dominated the social and political scene of Algeria—"French Algeria." They discriminated against the natives.

As you may envisage, the majority of Muslims were poor and illiterate. The French army had tight hold on Muslim population, and was ready to quell any rebellion arising from discontentment. It is worth noting here that besides Algeria, France also colonized neighbouring Tunisia and Morocco before the First World War. To be sure, Algeria was a divided world of the native and the colonizer, of the exploiter and the oppressed, of racial tensions, of the rich and paupers, of the haves and have-nots, of the well-fed and the hungry. It contained the seeds of explosion.

In section 3 we discussed the problem of alienation of the colonized as Fanon describes it. Fanon describes the social and political condition of Algeria with reference to the alienation of the natives in most of his major works: *A Dying Colonialism, Toward the African Revolution,* and *The Wretched of the Earth.* The natives were deprived of full social and political rights. Attempts spearheaded by nationalist leaders had been made to improve the situation by social and political reforms.[54] French assimilative policy was considered as a viable option for attaining these goals by some of these leaders who came from the emerging middle class consisting of intellectuals groomed in French schools, army officers and leaders appointed by the French government. The aspiration of these leaders was to become French citizens. They acted as mediators between the colonial masters and the natives who disparagingly called them *"Beni Oui Oui,"* (A Breed of Yes-Men). Since they were profiting from the colonial system, they could not really represent the aspirations of the natives so as to form the vanguard of the rising Algerian nationalism. The attainment of French Citizenship by some of them did not mean equality of rights with the Europeans.

However, for the mass of the natives the condition of alienation remained. The European population in Algeria organized itself into a very powerful front for gaining social and political rights and privileges, and for nullifying any movements for equal rights with the natives. They rejected and looked down upon French-educationed Muslims.

The tide of Algerian nationalism could not be stifled. It found expression in the emergence of various political movements with corresponding attitudes to French assimilative policy. When in 1936 Blume-Viollette Bill was proposed for granting French citizenship to some Algerian Muslims, Ferhat Abbas who had been agitating for French citizenship for all Algerians supported it, while Messali Hadj, the leader of ENA[55] which espoused the cause of independent Algeria opposed it. The Association of Algerian Ulema (religious teachers) which was opposed to the dominance of French culture, and wanted to have Arabic as the official language of Algeria was more cautious and pragmatic than ideological in supporting the bill. Unfortunately, the bill fell through under the pressure of conservative and business fronts in France and of European mayors in Algeria.

The French Communist Party which had given support to ENA in its bid for Algerian equality and freedom within the

French hegemony withdrew support; this was a fatal blow, and ENA was officially dissolved by the Popular Front Government. Embittered by this experience, the leader of the ENA, Massali Hadj renounced the French Communist Party together with its Marxist ideology, and espoused the cause of Pan-Arabism (PPA) which became a nationalist party with a substantial support from the working class in France and Algeria.[56] It may be remarked that the failure of the Blume-Violette program destroyed the trust of assimilationists, and raised great doubts as to the validity of assimilation itself. To some people assimilation reflects nothing but the depersonalization of the natives, and consequently, could not be a good and lasting solution to the colonial problem. Furthermore, the bitter experience of associating with various French political parties resulted in the emergence of splinter political parties, with some moderating in favour of social, political and economic reforms, and others radicalized in favour of complete independence for Algeria.

With the ascendance of the Vichy Government after the fall of France in 1940 came the banning of all Algerian political parties, the incarceration of some of their leaders and the curtailment or deprivation of some of the Muslim political gains. It strongly favoured the Europeans in Algeria.

However, the nationalists continued undaunted in their aspirations despite heavy odds. Disillusioned by the intransigence of the Vichy Government, Ferhat Abbas presented an Algerian Manifesto demanding complete independence for Algeria. But, the French Committee of National Liberation, headed by General de Gaulle and General Girand in 1943 rejected it, and instead proposed that French citizenship be granted to certain classes of Muslims while still retaining their Muslim status. It looked as if half a loaf of bread is better than none. The Committee's proposal appeared liberal enough but condescending. It failed to satisfy the demands of the nationalists. However, Ferhat Abbas continued to work for a peaceful settlement of the colonial problem. The Algerian situation was gradually heading to a crisis as nationalist leaders were divided as to whether to allow events to evolve into a peaceful settlement within the French framework or to force a resolution by revolution.

The crisis was reached on the eventful day, 8th of May, 1945, when amid celebrations of the Allied powers for their victory in ending the war, a procession of the members of the Messali and Abbas parties had a confrontation with the police in the town of Setif. Despite the appeal for calm by Abbas, emotions ran high in the nationalist demonstration. The origin of the riot which then broke out has remained unknown. Shots fired by the police left many dead, including some innocent people. The nationalists attacked some Europeans by way of revenge and about 103 Europeans were killed and 110 wounded.[57] Fearing a nationalist uprising, the French authorities made a sweeping counterattack which took a heavy toll of about 40,000 Muslims.[58] The events at Setif symbolized the irreconcilability of the colonist mentality with the human aspirations of the natives to equality. They drove a wedge of separation into the nerve centre of the colonial system; and subsequent events demonstrated the logic of the dialectics of colonial imperialism and decolonization.

In 1947, an Algerian statute was introduced by the French National Assembly. It created a two-college assembly representing two Algerian separate communities, Europeans and Muslims. Although it was a controversial statute, it was liberal enough to enlist the support of the majority of Muslims. Accordingly, elections were scheduled for April 1948. Fearing the prospect that the Muslims would have a majority in the new Algerian Assembly, the Europeans put pressure to avoid that prospect by having the elections rigged. To perpetuate European dominance in the Algerian political scene, "later elections of 1951, and 1953 were similarly 'arranged.'"[59] As Irene L. Gendzier has remarked, "It is a sad commentary on the possibilities that existed but remained unrealized, that legal methods of change were tested without success. It was not for lack of effort on the Algerian side, and for this the political biography of Abbas is the most convincing piece of evidence."[60]

Frantz Fanon was greatly moved by the lack of proper response on the part of the French Government and people to the deteriorating situation in Algeria. He poignantly posed the problem of the Algerian situation in this *Letter to a Frenchman*. It reflects the misery of the Arab and the cloak of silence and neglect of his fellow man, the Frenchman:

When you told me you wanted to leave Algeria . . . I was looking at you and at your wife beside you . . .

You told me that the atmosphere is getting rotten, I must leave.

How inexplicably the country bristles. The roads no longer safe. The wheat fields transformed into sheets of flame. The Arabs becoming hostile.

People talk. People talk.

The women will be raped . . .

Remember Setif. Do you want to see another Setif?

They will, but we won't.

All this you told me, laughing.

But your wife wasn't laughing.

And behind your laugh I saw.

I saw your essential ignorance of this country and its ways . . .

. . .

Perhaps you will leave, but tell me, when you are asked,

'What is going on in Algeria?' What will you answer?

. . .

When people want to know why you left this country, what will you do to stifle the shame that already burdens you?

The shame of not having understood, of not having wanted to understand what has happened around you every day.

. . .

And no part of this enormous wound has pushed you in any way.

. . .

Concerned about Man but strangely not about the Arab.

. . .

For there is not a European who is not revolted, indignant, alarmed at everything, except at the fate to which the Arab is subjected.

Unperceived Arabs.

Ignored Arabs.

Arabs passed over in silence.

Arabs spirited away, dissimulated.

Arabs daily denied, transformed into the Saharan stage set.

And you mingling with those:

Who have never shaken hands with an Arab.

Never drunk coffee.

Never exchanged commonplaces about the weather with an Arab.

By your side the Arabs.

Pushed aside the Arabs.

Without effort rejected the Arabs.

Confined the Arabs.

Native town crushed.

Town of sleeping natives.

. . .

All this leprosy on your body.

You will leave, but all these questions, these questions without answer. The collective silence of 800,000 Frenchmen, this ignorant silence, this innocent silence.

And 9,000,000 men under this winding sheet of silence.

. . .

I want my voice to be harsh . . .

I want it to be torn through and through, I don't want it to be enticing, for I am speaking of man and his refusal, of the day-to-day rottenness of man, of his dreadful failure.

. . .

Listen further:

. . .

A schoolmistress complaining that once all the Europeans were enrolled, she was obliged to give schooling to a few Arab children.

. . .

Teach the Arabs? You're not serious. So you just want to complicate our lives. They're fine the way they are. The less they understand the better off they are.

. . .

Millions of young bootblacks. Millions of *"porter, madam?"*

Millions of give me a piece of bread.

Millions of illiterates *"*not knowing how to sign, don't sign, let us sign.*"*

Millions of fingerprints on the police reports that lead to prisons.

On Monsieur le Cadi's[62] records.

On the enlistments in the regiments of Algerian infantry.

Millions of *fellahs*[63] exploited, cheated, robbed. *Fellahs* grabbed at four in the morning, released at eight in the evening.

. . .

Fellah gorged with water, gorged with leaves, gorged with old biscuit which has to last all month.

. . .

Arabs on the roads.

Sticks slipped through the handle of the basket.

Empty baskets, empty hope, this whole death of the *fellah*.

Two hundred fifty francs a day.

Fellah without land.

Fellah without reason.

. . .

Six times two hundred fifty francs a day.

And nothing here belong to you.

We're nice to you, what are you complaining about?

What would you do without us? A fine country this would be if
we left!

. . .

Work *fellah*. In your blood the prostrate exhaustion of a whole
lifetime.

Six thousand francs a month.

On your face despair.

In your belly resignation . . .

What does it matter *fellah* if this country is beautiful.[64]

The details of the above quotation show how alienation was
pervasive among the native population in Algeria. It was this
which prompted Fanon to tender his letter of resignation[65]
from the psychiatric hospital of Blida-Joinville. Since it is the
aim of psychiatry to overcome the alienation of the individual
in the personal and social spheres of living, it is necessary to
minimize or eliminate the causes of mental disorientation in
the social system if psychiatric treatment is to be successful.
It is unavailing where the system is ridden with corruption
that stifle human aspirations and values. By his activities
Fanon hoped for the emergence of a better world which can be
frustrated by an institutionalized contempt of man. He felt the
condition of the Arab who has been made into a thing with no
opportunity of realizing his human aspirations. As Fanon remarks, "The social structure existing in Algeria was hostile
to any attempt to put the individual back where he belonged."
Deprived of his human dignity, and left at the mercy of colonial
opportunism and exploitation, the poor Arab goes about his
endless daily rounds without a future. Fanon believes that a

social structure is meant to serve human needs, and when warped with corruption, it "drives its members to desperate solution," and consequently it atrophies and should be replaced. The problem of lawlessness, inequality and murders can only be solved when sincere efforts are made at the human level and not when they are covered with a veneer of legitimacy. Fanon also maintains that the strikers on July 5, 1956 had a legitimate cause, and that the punitive measures against them was unreasonable.

In order to avoid a cynical attitude, Fanon resigned his post in protest as a matter of conscience, because he thought that the future would not absolve those who were privileged with knowing the truth but failed to speak out, and preferred to remain passive. As a humanist, he now faces up to the problem of changing the situation in Algeria. Is turning revolutionary with the risk of using violence the appropriate option? In the following chapter we shall discuss his dilemma as a humanist in justifying the use of violence to relieve oppression since colonialism is fundamentally inexcusable, and no one can enslave another as a matter of principle.

Chapter IV

CRITICAL PRINCIPLES: JUSTIFYING VIOLENCE

1. FANON'S DILEMMA

In the face of the crisis situation described in the preceding chapter, a genuine humanist may either take active measures which may include the use of violence in order to terminate the condition of alienation of the colonized or oppressed or leave things as they are for fear of violating humanistic values by using revolutionary means which necessitate the use of violence. This is the typical dilemma of any would-be-reformer or revolutionary. It is the point of Levi's comment that from Socrates, Plato, and the stoics, to the humanists of the twentieth century there has been "the permanent dialectic of embracement and rejection, the ceaseless ballet of advance and withdrawal before the political arena."[1] I think that Fanon was in a dilemma when he opted for the use of revolutionary violence in order to terminate the alienating condition of the colonized in view of his "new humanism."

The need here is to establish critical principles on which to base the justification of his espousal of violence, and thereby destroy the charge against him; in other words, what kind of critical framework can we advance in order to reconcile his espousal of violence with his humanism? Or are they irreconcilable?

Such a critical framework is provided by the principle of self-defense, and the principle of double effect. Fanon does not explicitly mention or use these principles, but he can avail himself of them in order to reconcile his espousal of violence with his humanism. Thus, we want to look at his conception of revolution as a means of self-defense on the part of the colonized or oppressed.

Within the context of evaluating Fanon's revolutionary humanism in view of the use of violence, I think that the principle of self-defense and the principle of double effect are not entirely independent of each other, but rather are mutually reinforcing. As we shall see, the principle of double effect reinforces the principle of self-defense, because, even when it is justifiable to use appropriately effective force which may be deadly in order to defend oneself from an unjust attack, the killing of another human being or the use of violence against him is not at best a good but a necessary evil which should not be willed. This is so, because a humanism of Fanon's stance which has a universalist thrust, is committed somehow to loving even the enemy.

The crucial issue is that of justifying violence in forms such as torture, killing, bombing, terrorism, killing the innocent, and destruction of property in the attempt to resolve the crisis situation of the preceding chapter. The problem arises where violence, as described above, appears to be necessary. We shall attempt to show in what sense it can be justified. Here, I think that it is necessary to introduce the discussion by making a few remarks on violence in view of the critical framework.

2. REMARKS ON VIOLENCE

From the outset, we should like to exclude from our consideration the arbitrary use of violence; that is, violence that is done for "enjoyment." This would have no rational justification, and is intrinsically evil in the sense that it negates the human dignity of the victim which authentic humanism espouses. If the revolutionary has no qualms about using violence at any time, he is guilty of arbitrariness, because there would be, at least, no rational control of the situation by balancing means and ends, and by weighing the consequences of the revolutionary violence in terms of seeing whether the suffering of the victims, innocent or otherwise, is offset by the better condition. For violence in any form to be justified, it must be envisioned as controllable and capable of being stopped at a point of strict necessity, otherwise, it becomes arbitrary and lacks the sense of being imputable to the perpetrator, and therefore, is incompatible with the spirit of authentic humanism which is concerned about anything that tends to injure the respect due to the human person. For the revolutionary to "act," he must somehow determine how far he can go; he must therefore, have qualms at times, and use restraint in the use of violence.

The problem of controlling the use of violence becomes more complicated when considered in view of the fact that violence is characterized by chain reaction. When one is frustrated by the use of violence, one often reacts by trying to frustrate the frustration or counter it by more violence; and violence perpetuates, unless one comes to realize that it is unavailing in the face of greater violence. An atmosphere of violence makes it easy for people to be habituated to violence. Where violence is seen to pay, and is institutionalized, there is the tendency to get through one's way by resorting to violence. However, violence may play a role in the elimination of violence. Since violence tends to degrade the victim, the respect due to a rational nature, the use of violence in itself is restricted. Hence, the problem of its moral justification. This is the point of the argument on the principle of self-defense, and on the principle of double effect to which we shall now direct our attention. However, the justification of violence, and especially revolutionary violence in a particular case, must take into account the characteristic of chain-reaction of violence.

3. SELF-DEFENSE

Since, as we have remarked, violence tends to degrade the victim, it is not easy to find a just and legitimate use of violence in view of an authentically universalist humanism. It is generally acknowledged that a paradiamatic case of a just or legitimate use of violence is that of self-defense. This case rests on the idea that one acts on the principle of respect for human life.

If a man is unjustly attacked, he has the right to defend himself; that is, to defend his right to life, to freedom, to the use of his mental and physical members and powers. For the notion of right implies the use of appropriate means to defend it in the case of an attack. Self-defense may involve the use of appropriately effective force which may result in injury or death of the aggressor.

The phrase "appropriately effective force" is crucially important. It forestalls arbitrariness and recklessness in employing force which results in injury as counteraction against attack. It limits it to what is really necessary. For example, if A unjustly attacks B with the intention of injuring B, B is justified in defending himself by resisting with equal force which will make A incapable of getting his way. Where A intends to kill B, B may defend himself by force which may incapacitate A even to the point of killing A as the last resort. But if B could prevent A's intention in the struggle by only incapacitating A by maiming him, it would be inappropriately effective or even unjust for B to kill A outright. But if B does not realize that he need not kill A, his ignorance is an extenuating element in assessing his responsibility and culpability. Self-defense in an attack is a delicate situation which requires the rightful balancing of means and ends in view of the respect due to a human being.

But is B bound to defend himself? One may argue that the law of self-preservation dictates that a man use the necessary means to protect himself. Human life is a basic value to which commitment is appreciably a characteristic of being truly human. Although a man may give up his life to save another's, at bottom, he must appreciate his own life, and take safeguards in the event of trying to save another's. This is a case of love for another. A man who has a family to provide for may be doing an act of injustice to his family if he does not defend himself from an unjust attack that will disable or kill him. Violence in self-defense is justifiable with the proviso that it is limited to what is strictly necessary in order to restrain an attack. The latter provision is a necessary condition, because the use of violence against another is something to be deplored even though justifiable and should not be excessive.

Since violence tends to injure human dignity, it may be asked whether it is morally justifiable against an unjust aggressor on the ground that, by employing violence unjustly against another, he forfeits the right that forbids violence done to him as a rational creature, and consequently may be restrained by any necessary means. This would mean that a person's right forbidding violence to be done to him is not absolute but is predicated on his behaving rationally. Although debatable, this is plausible.

In this context, the remark of St. Thomas Aquinas to the objection that it is in itself evil to kill human beings is relevant:

> By sinning man departs from the order of reason, and consequently falls away from the dignity of his manhood, in so far as he is naturally free, and exists for himself, and he falls into the slavish state of the beasts, by being disposed of according as he is useful to others . . . Hence, although it be evil in itself to kill a man so long as he preserves his dignity, yet it may be good to kill a man who has sinned, even as it is to kill a beast. For a bad man is worse than a beast. and is more harmful.[2]

Aquinas used this argument for justifying capital punishment with regard to public jurisdiction.

However, one can argue, and rightly so as Germain G. Grisez does, that a person does not lose his innate human dignity when he behaves irrationally by wrongdoing:

> Of course, a person does in some sense degrade himself by wrongdoing. Yet such self-degradation, even if it is conceived as a kind of existential suicide, cannot alter one's human nature or detract from one's inherent dignity as a human person. Our consensus today surely would be that if we treat even the worse criminals as if they were animals (or worse than animals) we brutalize ourselves and dishonor our humanity.
>
> Each good that is intrinsic to the human person participates in the dignity of the person, a dignity that is beyond calculable price and measurable worth. Goods *for* man can be priced; goods *in* man can only be prized.[3]

The text of Aquinas' comment is rather ambiguous, as Donagan has pointed out, in view of what Aquinas said about killing in self-defense.[4] To clear the ambiguity of the text, one may interpret it by saying that it may mean either that by sinning, a man loses his human dignity by being totally corrupt or that by sinning, he does not totally lose his human dignity because he is only partially corrupted by abusing his freedom which is his as a rational creature; that is, "by violating the order of reason," as Donagan put it, "he falls from a state in which his freedom among other free men must be respected, and may without prejudice to his human dignity be subjected to coercion in order to protect others." This coercion extends to killing him to defend the lives of those he attacks. This accords with the Christian tradition that human nature is not totally corrupted by sin.

It means that one's irrational behaviour by wrongdoing does not reduce one to the complete negation of rationality or to the irrational. Hence, the principle of self-defense which dictates the use of appropriately effective coercive means which may result in the injury or death of the aggressor does not negate *per se* the human dignity of the aggressor or oppressor; and therefore self-defense on this ground is morally justifiable.

In order to obviate the difficulty of negating the dignity of the aggressor or oppressor in self-defense, many authors advance the principle of double effect We shall consider this later. In the next chapter we shall consider how Fanon deals with the problem of the irrational behaviour of the oppressors, and how he may have presupposed the forfeiture of the immunity to violence on the part of the oppressor as a basis of justifying the use of violence on the part of the oppressed or colonized.

Can the principle of self-defense be justifiably extended to the group or state, as it were, to the individual or microcosm written large? The concept of "self" is a subject or a *locus* of rights. The problem is to show in a particular case that a group is a *locus* of rights. A group or political organization becomes a self by legitimation. Legitimation can come about by tradition (custom) or by consent. For example, an ethnic group acquires legitimation by the consent or agreement of the constituents. Although one may hold that the group is a self by analogy to the individual person, what is necessary to the concept of self is that it be a subject or *locus* of rights. As a self, it can defend itself by using appropriate force which may even result in violence.

There are important differences between the self of an individual and the self of the group or state. The action and power of an individual are less than that of the group or state. The problem of self-defense at the level of the group or state may involve the problem of civil wars, international wars, and wars of liberation or revolution. The problem here is that of controlling the means of defense, force. The danger of using excessive force which may result in excessive injury or destruction is greater in the defense of the group or state. In the case of self-defense on the part of an individual, the danger of excessive use of force is somehow safeguarded by the fact that the individual can have recourse to the civil court or police for redress and protection of his rights. This safeguard against excessive use of force is more or less absent in the case of groups or states which may try to settle their conflict by having recourse to more violence in the effort to restrain the force of the aggressor or oppressor. The danger of violent chain reaction is greater here. However the individual as well as the group or the state can be unjustly attacked, and so the group or the state may justly defend itself just as an individual can

One of the crucial issues raised by the defense of the group or state is that the lives of innocent people may be involved. Would it be right to include all members of a group, political or otherwise, as unjust aggressors when the decision is taken by representatives and, therefore, it would be justifiable to attack the civilian and military alike as a matter of self-defense? This raises the issue of the extent of responsibility on the part of the individual members of the group in bringing about the conflictual situation. This helps in the determination of who the innocent are. The question then arises whether it is ever justifiable to kill the innocent. Let us first see who the innocent may be on the side of the aggressors.

4. THE INNOCENT

(i) Who are the Innocent?

Traditionally speaking, the innocent are the noncombatants in a war, that is, the civilian population. The innocent in this sense include the children, the sick, the aged, nurses, doctors, farmers, shopkeepers, traders, dissenters, and those not bearing arms, but are causally connected with the war or the crisis situation. The latter includes manufacturers of machines of war, transporters, and food suppliers to the combatants. The leaders who decide on the war may not be regarded as innocent even though they are non-combatants. Manufacturers of the machines of the war risk the danger of not being innocent. Those who supply provisions, for example, food, clothing to the combatants also risk the danger of not being innocent, since they play a part in keeping the machine of war or oppression going. However, these are innocent in a qualified sense.

We may also mark out those who are forced to play their part for fear of incurring severe penalties in a general conscription. If these bear arms, and are combatants, they are not "innocent" because they can shoot and injure the "enemy." We may distinguish a situation in which the civilian population support the war effort by their enthusiasm and propaganda from a situation in which some support and some are opposed. Since it is not easy to draw the line with regard to civilian divisions in this matter, it is morally sound to regard the civilian population as "innocent" unless it is factually proven otherwise.

(ii) Killing the Innocent

The morality of a war of liberation or revolution is often judged by the fact that the innocent are or may be killed. Is it ever justifiable to kill the innocent? One view is that it is absolutely wrong to kill the innocent, and regards the killing of the innocent in a war or revolutionary situation as murder.[5]

One must distinguish direct and indirect killing of the innocent. Direct killing of the innocent is to intentionally perform an action that of its very nature brings about the death of the innocent. For example, shooting point blank at the innocent will cause the death of the innocent.

By indirect killing of the innocent is meant to do an action that is not of its very nature and intentionally meant to bring about the death of the innocent, but the death of the innocent follows as a result among other results which are the aim of the doer. For example, a doctor who performs an abortion by intentionally cutting the vital links of a nonviable fetus with the mother directly kills the innocent fetus; but if he were to administer certain drugs that have the effect of curing the sick pregnant woman, and the death of the fetus results as a side effect, he would be killing the innocent fetus indirectly. There is a great moral difference between the two actions and results.

In a given war or revolutionary situation, shooting the innocent point blank is direct killing; and shooting at combatants as a target in which stray bullets kill the innocent which is not intended is indirect killing. Where obliteration bombing, for example, is conducted, and innocent people are killed, the action would be direct killing, because the great power of destruction released, by its nature, would not be selective and would consume both the combatants and the innocent.[6]

It can be argued that a timed bombing of a gathering place with a timely warning to the occupants would not be direct killing of the innocent, if some of the occupants are killed and their death is not intended but only the destruction of the resort area.

With regard to the direct killing of the innocent, one might ask in what sense it is absolutely forbidden to kill the innocent. Is the sense of "absolutely" *prima facie* in the absolutist view, or is it strictly absolute; that is, is it always immoral in all circumstances to kill some innocent persons directly even to save more innocent persons?

A moderate view would take "absolutely" in the *prima facie* sense; that is, in general it is forbidden to kill the innocent directly, but under certain circumstances, for some overriding reason, for example, the preservation of more lives, of innocent lives, or freedom of the oppressed can justify the killing of the innocent. This would mean that the benefit of the doubt will be given to the innocent, and the burden of providing the gravest justificatory reasons will be on the perpetrator. But the problem with the moderate view is that it regards human life which is imponderable, incalculable and priceless as calculable and quantifiable, and so the view rests on utilitarian grounds. It regards some lives more valuable than others, and so a few lives may be disposed of in order to save a greater number; and this is supposed to result ultimately in the happiness of a greater number who will live.

In view of genuine humanism, one wonders if a humanist with a universalist ethical thrust may consistently take the utilitarian stance. I do not think that he can do so because of the basic attitude of calculating and quantifying human life in the utilitarian theory. Consequently, I think, a genuine humanist can justify the killing of the innocent persons only if it is indirect in a particular case, under the gravest of circumstances, because the innocent have the right of life even in a revolutionary situation. Intentional killing of an innocent person is murder. Indiscriminate killing is immoral. The paradigmatic ground for the justifiable use of violence which is deadly is self-defense.

5. THE PRINCIPLE OF DOUBLE EFFECT

Since human life has intrinsic value, the killing of another human being, to say the least, is an evil. To justify it under certain circumstances one must regard it as a "necessary evil." A classic principle that minimizes the evil of killing another human being is the principle of double effect, which Catholic theologians in the seventeenth century developed from the justification of killing in self-defense advanced by St. Thomas Aquinas.[7] An appeal is often made to this principle in justifying the killing of another human being in self-defense.

In a nutshell, the principle of double effect expresses the following points: A person is justified in performing an action which gives rise to a good effect and a bad one. He is not morally held responsible for the bad effect if (1) the action is not vitiated on some other account, (2) the person does not will the bad effect either in itself or as a means to the good effect, (3) there is a right intention on the part of the person, and (4) the person has a reason proportionately grave for doing the action and permitting the occurrence of the bad effect.[8]

This principle encapsulates a sophisticated moral experience and should be applied with caution. Although it is a practical guide for solving morally perplexing cases, it requires "sound moral judgments" to avoid the abuse of sophistical applications.

Because the principle of double effect bristles with the danger of being abused with regard to the avoidance of willing a bad result which is foreseen, some writers have abandoned it or criticized it as presupposing the Cartesian psychology in which intentions are "produced at will" and directed or withdrawn at will in order to avoid willing the bad result as a means.[9] According to them, this is a pretense in that it is psychologically impossible for one honestly to avoid willing a bad result which follows immediately one's action if one foresees that the result would inevitably follow. They claim that the intending of means as such is necessarily bound up with one's actions. Hence, they reject the principle of double effect as a justification of killing in self-defense, because they maintain that it is impossible for one to avoid intending the deadly force required for successful self-defense as a means.

As we can see, the second requirement, namely, that the agent should not will the bad effect either in itself or as a means to the good result is the crux of the principle of double effect. It has become the bone of contention among some well known authors, such as Peter Knauer, S.J., W. Van der Marck, O.P., and Germain Grisez, who have criticized it in order to formulate a theory of killing that is consonant with the dictates of the Natural Law.

To clear the perplexity and difficulty in the second requirement, Knauer reinterprets the idea of directness: "I say that an evil effect is not 'directly intended' only if there is a 'commensurate ground' for its permission or causation. One may permit the evil effect of his act only if he has a commensurate reason for it."[10] According to him, the moral quality of an act is determined by the reason given for it, that is, whether the reason is commensurate or not. As he puts it, "Moral evil, I contend, consists in the last analysis in the permission or causing of a physical evil which is not justified by a commensurate reason."[11] This means that "a commensurate reason" makes the intention of a bad result indirect and redeems an action which would otherwise be bad. He does not equate "commensurate reason" with "serious reason." In his view, "The principle of double effect means that to cause or permit an evil without a commensurate reason is a morally bad act."[12]

However, the main difficulty with Knauer's theory is how to determine commensurate reason in particular cases, and for that matter in some hard cases. For example, he was asked by the editor who translated his article whether a woman may commit adultery in order to have her children rescued from a concentration camp.[13] Would her adulterous act be morally good since she has a "commensurate reason?" Knauer does not give a positive answer but says:

The question must be answered in relation to the whole context.

> Does life or freedom have any value if in the end one is forced
> to give up all human rights and in principle be exposed to every
> extortion? This would be in contradiction to the very values of
> life and freedom.[14]

The point is that it is hard to justify an adulterous act under
such circumstances and Knauer's theory does not give adequate
guidance in such a hard concrete case. Knauer's 'commensurate
reason' appears to be a hedge of ambiguity.

Van der Marck's criticism of the principle of double effect
rests on his reinterpretation of human act which he regards
as "a unique reality," because it has physical and spiritual aspects. "It is neither pure intention nor a purely material physiological reality. Rather, it is a combination of both . . ."[15] Accordingly, his view avoids pure spiritualism and materialism.

Furthermore, he maintains that a human act is essentially
intersubjective in that it refers to the delicate balance of the
community. It is "community-forming or community-breaking
—it makes for community relationship, or rejects it;"[16] hence
it is "good" or "evil" respectively. According to him, the positive and negative effects of a human act depends "on the concrete requirements of the community here and now." In other
words, the community-building or community-breaking quality
is relative to the actual situation of the community in point,
for "that which is community-forming here today can be com-
munity-destroying some where else tomorrow."[17]

Van der Marck also holds that "act," "means," "end," "intention," or "purpose" form an indivisible unity in the integrity
of a concrete human act; the physical performance (material
act) gets its human significance from the intention. The moral
quality of a human act is ultimately derived from intersub-
jectivity, that is, from its overall effect with reference to community-forming or community-breaking. In his view, means or
ends (intentions) are not said to be good or bad apart from "actual realization" and human acceptance. What can be said to be
good or bad is a human act.

Accordingly, he rejects the principle of double effect on the
ground that it is based on a misconception of human act in
which each physical performance (act) is regarded as a human
effect and consequently can be considered as a good or bad
means, whereas it is not, since its human effect is with respect
to the community-building or community-disruption.[18] Furthermore, he rejects it on the ground that it is based on a "materialis-
tic (and ultimately, dualistic) conception" of human action.[19]

Thus, in his example of transplantation, the physical mutilation in view of transplanting an organ or a part of a person's body to another is not a human act by itself but it constitutes a material substratum of the transplantation which is intended and humanly accepted, and consequently forms a human act. In the traditional view of the principle of double effect, the physical mutilation would have been said to be intended and would have been a human act and a bad means to transplantation; but according to Van der Marck the physical mutilation is not a separate human act; it is merely a material substratum of the human act of transplantation.

However, I think that Grisez's criticism of Van der Marck's rejection of the principle of double effect as unjustifiable is in place. As Grisez points out, "Van der Marck is mistaken in drawing the conclusion that there cannot be a morally bad means to a good end."[20] Individual intentions of the agent are important factors in the morality of the performance and not just the overall effects of the act on the community. "One who makes a tool (means) in order to use it (end) can exploit slave labour to make the tool (bad means) in order to use it."[21] Furthermore, Van der Marck's theory is susceptible to a totalitarian interpretation in that any action, which, considered as a whole, makes for the good of the community could easily be justified. For example, using slave labour for ameliorating the material conditions of a community would be justified on his theory. In the same vein, the liquidation of a minority for the overall good of a community would be justified. Here the smack of utilitarianism in his theory is apparent.

In the light of the preceding discussions, we can see that the crux of the theory of human action in view of the principle of double effect, as Grisez points out, is how to determine the extent the natural cause of an effect can be viewed as a means in the moral domain. Grisez's criticism of the principle of double effect is directed to this problem.

Grisez argues that one's intentions and the "indivisibility of performance" are the elements which constitute the unity of a human action. He holds that "a performance considered as a process of causation in the order of nature includes not only the bodily movements of the agent, but also the inevitable effects which naturally follow from these movements."[22] On his showing, these various results can be the results of different actions depending on the doer intending them even though there is only one performance. Since the intention specifies a human action, he maintains that each result can be the end of an action if intended. The performance can be viewed as a matrix of different actions according as different effects are intended.

The point of Grisez's theory is to distinguish means and ends which are in the moral domain from cause and effect which are in the natural order. A performance can be means (moral) when it is intended, and an effect can be an end when intended. Bearing in mind the distinction between the moral order and the natural one, he argues that if the unity of action remains unimpaired and the intention specifying the action is good, the sequence of good and evil effects in the natural order does not matter in the moral order. From the moral standpoint, "all events in the indivisible performance of a unitary human act are equally immediate to the agent; none is prior (as means) to another."[23]

To illustrate his analysis of human action in view of the principle of double effect, Grisez gives the example of a mother who interposes herself between her child and an attacking animal. Here the performance of intervening is a unitary act from which two effects emanate, namely, saving the child, and the injury she incurs. She intends the effect of saving her child but not the injury which results from the intervention considered as a process of causation. But she could not commit adultery to save her child because the good effect of saving her child is not an immediate consequence from the adulterous performance. Here there is no unity of performance and effect, and the good effect of saving her child is a distinct human act. She would be intending the adulterous act as a means to the good end.[24]

Grisez argues against the justification of intentional killing because he maintains that human life is inviolable according to the dictates of the Natural Law. However, he justifies killing on the principle of self-defense reinforced by the principle of double effect. On the basis of his analysis, the only justification of capital punishment in some cases is self-defense on the part of the community, such as in a situation where a criminal has been offered the option of banishment or death. In the same vein, killing in self-defensive warfare is justifiable. Here the act of self-defense (performance) which is justifiable in itself is the cause of the good effect of preserving the life of the community and restraining the violence (unjust use of force) of the enemy and the bad effect of injuring or killing the enemy. Here the unity of performance and the two-fold effect is not broken. What is intended by the defender is the good effect which becomes the end of action while the bad effect is not intended, so does not constitute the end of action. Hence, Grisez holds that in a self-defensive war a soldier is justified in shooting at the enemy soldier (performance) in the battlefield to reduce the military capability of the enemy by one gun but without intending the killing of the enemy soldier (bad effect). The bombing of military installations (performance) to destroy or reduce the military force of the enemy (good effect) without intending the death of possible victims (bad effect) can be justified on the same ground. But non-military installations such as hospitals could not be bombed with clear conscience. It must be noted that, on the principle of double effect, it would be unjustifiable to kill the enemy soldier if he can be restrained otherwise, or if he has surrendered.[25]

Grisez's analysis is a helpful critical framework for dealing with Fanon's espousal of revolutionary violence. A war of liberation or revolution can be considered as a self-defense on the part of the colonized or oppressed. The force used to restrain the grip of oppression is justifiable on the principle of self-defense reinforced by the principle of double effect. The principle of double effect, as expounded by Grisez, makes it possible to obviate the difficulty of intending the injury or death of the oppressor while intending the safety and preservation of the oppressed (good effect) in the act or performance of self-defense which is in itself justifiable with the proviso which we have already indicated.

In view of Grisez's analysis, however, we may remark here that the natural consequences of a process of causation initiated by the human agent in the natural order must be taken into consideration even though its ramifications are not envisaged by the agent, because one can be held responsible for lack of care or ignorance. Where due consideration has been given to the facts in the process of causation in the natural order by the human agent, the balancing of the good effect from the point of view of the human agent, and of the evil effect from the viewpoint of the natural causation must be made. The performance may be considered as a neutral ground; the balance tips in favour of the good effect which is intended, if the evil effect is not overwhelming, but in favour of refraining from action if the evil effect is overwhelming. I think that the bad effect in view of the principle of double effect with regard to the first option may be considered as a necessary evil. This would be a case in which the chain reaction of violence is taken into account in a revolutionary situation.

You may have noted that the example which I gave of a doctor who aborts a fetus as a result of the medication which he gave to the pregnant mother is based on the principle of double effect. The doctor does not intend the violence done to the fetus but only the good effect of curing the mother. We also can see that the case of justifying obliteration bombing in which the innocent are killed does not squarely fit into the framework of justifying violence on the principle of double effect.

It is important to recall here the justification of violence against an aggressor who, by using violence against another rational creature (human being), forfeits his immunity to violence as a rational being (4 • 3). While he does not forfeit his human dignity which is innate, his freedom can be restrained from harming others by appropriate violence. Thus the espousal of violence on the part of the oppressed or colonized against the colonizers who unjustly use continued violence against them can be justified.

I think that the reconciliation of humanism and violence can only be adequately achieved through the principle of self-defense reinforced by the principle of double effect together with the above qualifications. Since violence tends to injure the respect due to a human being it is not a good which should be willed. It can only be tolerated or deplored. On the other hand, one has the right to protect oneself from an unjust attack by using appropriately effective force which may result in the injury or death of the aggressor. By combining the principle of self-defense and the principle of double effect as reinforcing each other, a genuine humanist can justify his use of force which may injure the aggressor to protect himself and group while not intending the injury or death of the victim (aggressor). Since it is evil to will evil, the humanist avoids willing the evil of the injury or the death of the aggressor. Thus, genuine humanism is barely reconcilable with violence on the principle of double effect. In a war of liberation which a humanist espouses as a means of self-defense at the group level, he may blow up the military installations of the oppressor and even shoot at the enemy in order to restrain the oppressive force of the enemy without intending the death of the enemy. A genuine humanist can therefore fight in a revolutionary war considered as a means of self-defense without contradiction of terms.

In view of the resolution of the problem of reconciling humanism and violence in a revolutionary or crisis situation, it is appropriate to discuss some particularly common forms of violence, namely, torture, terrorism in the light of the above principles.

6. TORTURE

In a given crisis or revolutionary situation those suspected as agents of the enemy, or prisoners are subjected to certain forms of violence to make them reveal some information about the movement, tactics, programs and other secrets relating to the internal and external security. Torture is a form of violence often used. Is torture justifiable for extracting the information? May torture be regarded as a means of self-defense?

Torture may take the form of flogging, beating, putting the feet in the stocks, using electrical appliances to cause physical pain on the victim. These may result in the attentuation of mental powers and temporary unconsciousness. Here there is a conflict between the right of the individual victim to decent treatment as a human being and perhaps the "right" of more people to have their lives preserved through the information which is extracted; for example, by obtaining the information about the enemy's military installations and programs of attack, the torturers may prevent the loss of lives or property by attacking military installations in the effort to incapacitate the enemy or evacuate by tactical maneuvers, or maintaining a better self-defense position.

One would have to distinguish the position of the oppressor or unjust aggressor from that of the oppressed or unjustly attacked. In the hands of the oppressor or the unjust aggressor, torture is a repressive measure to keep down the oppressed, and would not be morally justified. But in the hands of the oppressed or unjustly attacked it is plausible to consider it within the perimeter of self-defense where the rights of the oppressed, particularly innocent victims of a repressive system, are at stake. In this case it must not be arbitrary. The use of torture must not be based on mere suspicion, but on the certainty that the victim has the information. More importantly, the victim must be in a certain sense an "enemy" and not innocent. If an "enemy," the refusal of the victim to give the information can be regarded as a continual state of aggression where the information is necessary to incapacitate him and others of his party in order to prevent a continued attack. On this ground, the oppressed or attacked may regard torture, as I have qualified it, as a legitimate act of self-defense. On the principle of double effect, the confrontation with the victim ("enemy") who has the option of not undergoing the painful experience (bad effect) of the torture performance by freely giving out the necessary information can plausibly be regarded as a performance which has two effects, namely, the good effect of having the necessary information, and the bad effect of the pain or injury which is not intended by the oppressed. This appears to be stretching the principle of self-defense reinforced by the principle of double effect too far, but I think that it is plausible provided the torture is not carried beyond the point of necessity, and the victim completely dehumanized.

Since torture tends to degrade the victim and also the perpetrator, it can only be justifiable plausibly as the last resort to extract information in a crisis situation where the lives of many innocent people are at stake, if the victim would not give away the information without torturing. At best, I think, the justification of torture in a given crisis situation rests on the ground that there is a conflict of rights of the victim and of those who would have their lives preserved by the information in self-defense. It is plausible to consider the victim as having lost his right to total immunity to violence when he is an enemy (aggressor). Here the limited discomfort or suffering of the victim is less than that of those already killed or maimed by the enemy in a defensive war. However, the proviso is that care must be taken to be sure that the victim is causally connected with keeping the repressive machine or aggressive war going, and that he is not subjected to suffering more than it is necessary. It is always a delicate matter to use violence.

7. THE USE OF TERROR

Another form of violence which causes great concern in revolutionary situations is the use of terror or terrorism. To use terror is to cause pervasive fear by acts of violence calculated to pressure a person, a group or community. Usually dictatorial and oppressive systems are perpetuated by terror tactics. Those who spearheaded liberation movements in order to relieve oppression often espouse terrorism. For example, the Irish Republican Army (IRA), the Palestinian Liberation Organization (PLO), the National Liberation Front of Algeria (FLN), the Viet Con, Terror International, and a host of national liberation organizations in Africa, Asia, Latin America and Europe make a familiar reading in the use of terror to relieve oppression.

By terrorizing the population of the oppressor the leaders of the oppressed group hope to make the population put pressure on their government to fulfill the demands of the oppressed; terror tactics is also often aimed at the government officials to make it abandon its firm hold of power. In this context, terrorism can be seen as a struggle for power. We shall be mainly concerned with this form of violence in the hands of those who want to relieve oppression with regard to the justification of this kind of violence. However, the use of terror tactics by those who want to maintain their power in an oppressive system form a backdrop to the possibility of justifying the use of terror in the hands of the oppressed to relieve oppression.

In the hands of oppressors terrorism takes the forms of arbitrary arrests with incarceration often combined with denial of bail before trial, tortures, killings, trumped-up charges and kangaroo courts, protracted imprisonment, and surveillance of the citizens.[26] On the other hand, those who want to relieve oppression terrorize the oppressor by kidnapping, torture, killing, bombing, hijacking of planes, sabotage of production lines and power lines, bank robbery. Terrorists do not engage in open warfare but in guerrilla warfare with the oppressors because of disparity of power. They form an underground movement and conduct their guerrilla warfare on the hit and run basis usually from rural areas or from urban enclaves. Where the rural population is controlled by the enemy government, the leaders of the oppressed often terrorize them to pressure them to support the liberation cause. A foothold among the rural population is a vantage point from which the terrorists conduct guerrilla warfare against the enemy. Where there is power link among the rural inhabitants with the enemy government—for example, in the person of a village chief, the terrorists kill the chief and his henchmen as a means of breaking the power link. The Viet Cong terrorized the villages this way.[27] In bombing shopping centres and streets, the IRA, for example, wants to pressure the Irish and British population to demand a unified Ireland from the British. The FLN used terror tactics in the Algerian War to pressure the French colonial power to grant Algerian independence.

The problem with terrorism is that it is often directed against the non-combatants, the civilian population because of the disparity of military capability between the oppressed and the oppressor. Can violence in the form of terrorism on the part of the oppressed be morally justified?

To answer this question, one will have to distinguish the cases where innocent lives are involved from the cases where the agents of the oppressive system are concerned, and also the cases where damage is done only to property without the intention of killing; for example, where a bomb is planted to blow up a building after warning the inmates to evacuate. Agents of an oppressive system are not "innocent" since without them the oppressive machinery will grind to a halt, and so will be liable to terrorist attack. These include the army, the police and all those who are authority links from the grass roots, local chiefs, to the top government chiefs.

One will also have to distinguish terror tactics which result in death from those which are only a threat, for example, the kidnapping of the diplomats of the oppressive government on the part of terrorists who spearhead the liberation movement. Kidnappings and hijackings of airlines are often used by the terrorist group for getting the release of political prisoners. Since killing is the extreme form of violence, it is difficult to justify the killing of those kidnapped as a means of pressuring the official members of the oppressive system. Terror tactics can be regarded as a means of self-defense on the part of the oppressed or unjustly attacked where the non-combatant population of the enemy support the aggression or oppression. Violence which may result in death will have to be limited to those of the enemy who shoot to kill. However, care must be taken to limit self-defensive operation to what is strictly necessary with regard to the use of force which may result in injury. In such cases the injury or death of the enemy must not be intended in view of reconciling the humanism of the revolutionary movement and violence, particularly in a colonial system.

Indiscriminate terror tactics that strike at the lives of innocent victims, for example, children, the aged, the sick are against the common human decency which respects the right of the innocent to their life even in time of war. Without this safeguard, the terrorists would be turning their operation into a war of the jungle, which would contradict their moral stance of achieving freedom and human dignity for the oppressed. The moral ground of the position of the oppressed implies the underlying possibility of reciprocal acknowledgment of the right to decent treatment of the innocent. because the oppressed think themselves as "innocent." Consequently, there is a limit to the use of violence which tends to destroy the human dignity of the victim. The innocent would be immune to violence. Fanon was sensitive to this.

Even on political grounds, the killing of the innocent does alienate the sympathy and moral support of the outside world for the oppressed. Since the success of a war of liberation may largely depend on the support of the international community, revolutionaries take care not to do what may alienate at least a large segment of the outside support. Attack on the innocent may harden the oppressor to fight to the finish or harass it to

listen to the demands of the oppressed. Hence, attack on the innocent is a risky move on the part of the terrorists who think of
themselves as spokesmen and representatives of the oppressed.

However, terror tactics that do not directly aim at innocent
lives but have the effect of pressuring the powers-that-be in the
oppressive system to loosen the clutches of power and allow
for the freedom of the oppressed may be justified, on the principle of self-defense, in view of the unjust acts of violence committed against the oppressed people. For oppression is a form
of continued aggression. Since as a matter of history, power
often only acknowledges power, the oppressed may have to show
some force to indicate their grievances as the last resort; and
this may take the form of terror activity, as we have indicated
above. In this context, it is important to remember that it is
necessary to show in a given situation that the system is oppressive and unjust, and that there is reasonable ground of
success. Without this, there is the danger of alienated individuals
who want to make romantic or utopian heroes of themselves;
a wave of greater violence may ensue and destroy the chances
of establishing universal humanism.

It is very important to note here that violence is not
intrinsically evil. It would be so if evil when considered physically, psychologically, and morally. Compared with non-
violence as a means of achieving human goals, it is morally
inferior;[28] it should only be used as a last resort within the context of self-defense, and should never be absolutized. Violence
is ambivalent in that it can result in evil effects and good ones,
and in this sense, it may be said to be a *necessary* evil from
the moral point of view. This is why it has to be deplored even
though it can give rise to good effects. In the hands of the oppressor or unjust attacker, it becomes evil on all accounts, but
in the hands of the oppressed within the context of self-defense
it is a *necessary* evil which results in the good of defending
themselves, affirming their identity and freedom. In this sense
it has therapeutic effects, as Fanon holds. The physical and
psychological suffering or possible death of the unjust attacker
is evil from the physical and psychological point of view, but
not from the moral standpoint. This is permitted by a genuine
humanist. Hence those who credit Fanon with the view that
violence is good in itself contradict the universal thrust of his
humanism and the overall tenor of his words. Non-violence
will always be the richer and more lasting means for achieving
human potential than violence, because non-violence carries
the tincture of love which stands as the highest bond and means

of growth among humans.

We have established in this chapter that, on the principle of self-defense reinforced by the principle of double effect, humanism can be reconciled with a qualified use of violence. In the next chapter we shall discuss the resolution of Fanon's problem of reconciling his humanism with his espousal of violence in the light of the above principles. Since Fanon operates within a dialectical framework, we shall see how the above principles can be an integral part of the dialectics of his revolutionary humanism, and how the fact of the dialectical relation of humanism and violence is an additional but supportive justification of his espousal of violence. Furthermore, we shall see that in the light of reconciling Fanon's humanism and violence within the dialectical framework, the dialectic in Fanon takes moral values into account and not just freewheel with material condition as in Marx.

Chapter V
RESOLUTION

In the light of the preceding discussion on the philosophical framework we shall now see how to resolve the apparent contradiction in Fanon's revolutionary humanism with regard to his espousal of violence as a means of decolonization. We shall thereby clear him of Coser's charge that his vision is an evil and destructive vision. The problem is whether Fanon succeeds in reconciling his humanism with violence.

I think that the resolution hinges on considering decolonization or the liberation movement on the principle of self-defense in which revolutionary violence is a means. The justifiability of violence on the principle of self-defense reinforced by the principle of double effect shows that violence can be reconciled with humanism. On this ground, I think that Fanon's humanism can be reconciled with this espousal of violence. Furthermore, since Fanon operates within a dialectical framework, as I have indicated, the reconciliation is achieved through the principle of self-defense reinforced by the principle of double effect which operates within the dialectical framework. Hence in the reconciliation humanism and violence are somehow placed in a dialectical tension as violence mediates in the resolution of the contradictions of the colonial system in view of establishing universal humanism. The fact that humanism stands in a dialectical relation to violence is an additional but supportive justification to the principle of self-defense reinforced by the principle of double effect.

We have seen in the preceding chapter that the use of appropriately effective force that may result in injury (violence) on the principle of self-defense is morally justifiable both at the individual and group or state levels. We have also argued that Algeria was a legitimately instituted *locus* of rights from the point of view of the natives before the French colonization which started with the French invasion, with the expropriation of the native land to enrich the colonizers. The colonial system is a long-term state of aggression against the natives. As Fanon put it:

Colonization is the organization of the domination of a nation after military conquest.[1]

Hence, according to Fanon,

The war of liberation is not seeking for reforms but the grandiose effort of the people, which had been mummified, to rediscover its own genius, to reassume its history and assert its sovereignty.[2]

On the same note he writes:

Decolonization is a national liberation, national renaissance, the restoration of nationhood to the people.[3]

Fanon considers the war of liberation as a process in which the pseudo right of the colonial power to rule is called in question. France wanted to maintain a "French Algeria," and thereby perpetuate her occupation, but Algeria is not French.[4] To Fanon, there is a desparate need to restructure the social and political system which is maintained by force and violence. To put things right would involve "a program of complete disorder" from the view of the colonial power and colons.

As the Colonial system is ridden with force and violence, and consequently seethes with the alienation of the colonized, Fanon argues that the program of a new order in which the natives or oppressed will find freedom on the human level will involve violent confrontations as the colonial power insists on its "right" to rule by force of arms. In this sense, as Fanon projects, it becomes clear to the native that "the narrow world, strewn with prohibitions"[5] calls for the use of violence for changing the situation. Fanon writes from the experience of the French colonial policy in Algeria, and sees it as a military establishment, and so it had to be overcome by force. Where colonization is gained and maintained by force and violence, and where peaceful protests on the part of the natives against a policy of lack of universal suffrage have been ignored or rejected, or opposed by violence, one can easily see that only the use of force which may result in injury can lead to decolonization.

The dialectical opposition on the part of the colonized against the long-term state of aggression of the French colonial system and its consequent alienation found expression in the Algerian

Insurrection which suddenly started with an outburst of violence on the eventful night of October 31, 1954 with about "70 incidents of ambushing, bomb-throwing, attacks on police stations and buildings, arson and destruction."[6] Most of these incidents occurred in areas within the Aures Mountain. The revolutionary fighters in the engagement were about 2,000 strong. The leaders of the CRUA[7] claimed responsibility for the incidents.

In astonishment, French authorities thought that the incidents were the work of some groups of highwaymen (fellagh)[8] involved in a sedition, and who could not withstand a strong military operation. They failed to see that a conflagration has been ignited. And failing to read the signs of the time, the French Prime Minister, Mendes-France still clung to the idea of "French Algeria" in his uncompromising announcement. To understand his stubbornness, one must set it against the background of the French defeat at Dien Bien Phu in the Indochina, and of the political agitations which had ended in independence in both Morocco and Tunisia. He thought that giving up Algeria would be thought as a sign of weakness on the part of France, and also would be like an amputation of a vital organ since Algeria constituted a bastion of French foreign hold. Later on in the struggle, Germaine Tillion expressed this relationship by saying that France and Algeria were complementary enemies. Hence, it would be disastrous to France to lose Algeria.

Consequently, French authorities made an all-out move to quell the rebellion in Algeria by sending reinforcement of a parachute battalion consisting mainly of Indochina War veterans. On November 1, 1954 Algeria saw herself garrisoned by 56,600 French soldiers, and by April 1956 the number reached 250,000 strong.[9]

It is worth noting that Jacques Soustelle who had become Governor General of Algeria in January 1955 introduced reformatory measures. These measures were opposed by the conservative elements among the colons. However, Soustelle was more bent on controlling the activities of the FLN. Unfortunately, he eventually gravitated to the side of the colons and espoused their cause in Paris.

The FLN, on the other hand, remained undaunted in the cause of national liberation. It drew support even from political opponents who then saw the advantage of burying their political hatchet. By August 1956, it was claimed that the ALN, the military arm of the FLN had mustered about 50,000 men. The FLN made progress as it had increasing support from Algerian stuents and workers.

To meet the increasing tenseness of the situation, the French authorities established the forces of Order which was empowered to police the native population and crush the revolutionary movement. However, they angled for influence over the Algerian natives in order to dissuade them from supporting the "rebellion," and be attached to France. Time was to tell that this tactic was unavailing. Suspected members of the FLN were incarcerated, brutally tortured by the French territorial units in order to obtain information about the revolutionary movement. According to reliable sources the number of political prisoners in Algeria was more than 4,000 by July 1955.[10] On becoming the Resident Minister of Algeria in winter 1956, Robert Lacoste reiterated the indissoluble bond that made Algeria French. He failed to realize that his proposal for reform within the existing framework had come too late. It was to him that Fanon sent his letter of resignation. A meeting at Soummam was proposed; but two days before the meeting Lacoste announced the arrival of 200,000 more men from France as reinforcement for diffusing the tense situation. This action on the part of the French authorities took the nationalists by surprise, and made them doubt that the French authorities wanted a peaceful rather than military solution.

To overcome the disadvantage of unequal military capability, the revolutionary fighters adopted guerrilla tactics, infiltrated rural areas and cities, especially Algiers. From this vantage point, they gradually won the support of the native Algerians who eventually identified themselves with the cause of the national liberation as they saw that the territorial units were fiercely bent on crushing the "rebellion," that is, their aspiration of freedom and dignity in bloody raids.

The military situation climaxed in the Battle of Algiers, which lasted for nine months. Among the incidents that triggered the battle, the important ones were the execution of prisoners from the revolutionary group in June 1956, the bombing carried out by French terrorists in the Casbah, and their blowing up of a building in which a nationalist who attempted to kill some Europeans had lived. Many innocent Algerian lives perished in the blowing up, and many made homeless.[11] The nationalists countered the brutality and repression of the French terrorists by terrorism in the form of exploding bombs in cafes to liquidate marked individuals. These incidents sometimes took innocent lives. Both sides were engaged in revengeful acts of excessive violence.

The Forces of Order became more brutal in their determination to crush the underground establishment of the FLN in Algiers. Unscrupulous, they indiscriminately tortured suspects whether innocent or otherwise in a concerted effort to round up all the nationalist leaders.[12] The case of the torturing of a 22 year old Djamila Boupacha, a beautiful Algerian girl, shocked the world.[13] The revolutionary fighters would argue their case of using urban terrorism on the principle of self-defense at the group level as they counter-attacked the French territorial units in order to lessen or destroy the pressure of oppression. But their acts of excessive violence which sometimes took the form of revenge are unjustifiable.

Fanon was moved by the degeneration of the situation in Algeria. He was horrified by the gamut of terror tactics, torture, bombing, massacre used by the Forces of Order in their determination to crush the FLN and supporters, and so keep down the aspirations of the natives to political independence. He recounted particularly with deep sorrow the indiscriminate bombing of the native village of Sakiet Sidi Youssef by the French territorial units. The incident was a tragedy which drew a chain of bitterness; and it became a turning point in the war of oppression. It was revolting to some French people in Paris. It drove a divisive wedge into the French foreign policy. The incident pointed up what a colonial force could do in order to maintain itself in power.

Fanon regards as irresponsible the attitude of the French Government which allowed inhuman tortures to be perpetrated in Algeria by the territorial units. He considers the attempt to crush the Algerian rebellion in a bloody raid "as a succession of negations of man and an avalanche of murders." Even the Communist Party to which the Algerians looked up for support gave nothing but idle promises. Consequently, in the light of the experience of the reign of terror this disappointment moved Fanon and his liberation front to make a decision of no return. They decided not to compromise the struggle for independence, since the struggle on the markedly human level is one for human dignity and freedom. Fanon and the FLN urged the French Left "to fight to make the government of their country respect the values which we call the right of peoples to self-determination, recognition of the national will, liquidation of colonialism, mutual and enriching relations of free peoples,"[14] and respect the Frenchmen who courageously refuse to fight against the Algerian people because they see it as an unjust war against the right of a people to self-determination. But as France, supported by the intrigues of the colons (settlers) in Algeria insisted on its "right" to a French Algeria by force of arms, the natives had no other course than to confront it in the effort to liberate themselves. They can justify their move on the principle of self-defense against the French aggression.

As we have seen, force which results in injury in a situation of self-defense must be appropriately effective. In view of his humanism, Fanon is sensitive to this requirement. To him, violence as a means of liberation must be calculated and organized because only organized action helps in the structuring of consciousness.

This means that for violence to be appropriately effective it must be organized or calculated against consequences; that is, it must be controllable. As we have already indicated, the problem of revolutionary violence as a means of self-defense on the part of the oppressed who want to relive the condition of alienation is often a problem of control because of the large scale involvement of people and instruments of destruction. Fanon is sensitive to this problem.

Since violence can bring a chain reaction, Fanon discountenances arbitrary violence which is contrary to genuine humanism, because it negates the right of the human person to decent treatment. Violence can boomerang and recoil on the head of the perpetrator, since more violence can be used to counter it. It can have emotional effects on the perpetrator; for example, Fanon recounts the effects of revolutionary and counter-revolutionary violence in the chapter of *The Wretched of the Earth,* entitled "Colonial Wars and Mental Disorders." His case studies of some patients who had carried out tortures reveal that they had become victims of nightmares of torture.

Fanon sometimes puts the use of violence, in a certain sense, at the level of the irrational. He pictures the colonial world as a Manichean world where rational persuasion would be unavailing to change the power grip of the colonial forces.[15] He considers it as a world where there is a negation of human values, as a place where the colonizers and the forces behind them debase themselves by attacking the basic values of human dignity and freedom of the natives. Fanon seems to argue, by implication, that, at the level of the irrational, only the irrational can counter the irrational. According to this view, the enemy had become the incarnation of the irrational by using all forms of violence, and therefore must be restrained or overthrown by violence in order to protect the human values of the oppressed.

As I have indicated before, the enemy must not be reduced

to the level of the merely irrational, because this would mar any project of establishing a genuinely universalist humanism. Although he may have disgraced his human dignity by abusing his freedom, he still retains his inherent dignity as a human being, but loses his immunity to violence by committing acts of violence against others; and therefore in order to protect the human rights of others, he can be retrained by appropriately effective force which may injure him. On the principle of double effect, the defending native soldiers need not aim at killing the enemy but only at lessening their force. I think that this can be advanced as a source of Fanon's complex reaction to the use of violence as a means of decolonization. He does not will the killing of other human beings. He calls it a "disaster and inhumanity."[16]

A painstaking reading of Fanon reveals a complex character, a man in a dilemma, a man with a battle of conscience in view of the use of violence. Although violence may be necessary as a means of decolonization, he deplores it:

> No man's death is indispensable for the triumph of freedom. It happens that one must accept the risk of death in order to bring freedom to birth, but it is not lightly that one witnesses so many massacres and so many acts of ignominy.[17]

Commenting on the use of terror, he writes:

> The decision to kill a civilian in the street is not an easy one; and no one comes to it lightly. No one takes the step of placing a bomb in a public place without a battle of conscience.

> The Algerian leaders who, in view of the intensity of the repression, thought they could answer the blows received without any serious problems of conscience, discovered that the most horrible crimes do not constitute a sufficient excuse for certain decisions.[18]

The problem here is that the innocent may be involved. Hence at the beginning of the war of liberation, the National Liberation Front prohibited certain forms of action which are against the international code of war. Consequently, Fanon counsels that:

> In a war of liberation the colonized must win, but they must do so cleanly, without "barbarity."
>
> . . .
>
> An underdeveloped people must prove, by its fighting power, its ability to set itself up as a nation, and by the purity of every one if its acts, that is, even to the smallest detail, the

most lucid, the most controlled people. But this is all very difficult.[19]

As the situation became increasingly difficult, Fanon's attitude to terrorism seems to border at times on an existentially moral impasse. The question is "whether freedom was worth the consequences of penetrating into that enormous circuit of terrorism and counterterrorism?"[20] However, he seems to discountenance it:

No, it is not true that the Revolution has gone to the lengths to which colonialism has gone. But we do not on this account justify the immediate reactions of our compatriots. We understand them, but we can neither excuse them nor reject them.

Because we want a democratic and a renovated Algeria, because we believe one cannot rise and liberate one's self in one area and sink in another, we condemn, with pain in our hearts, those brothers who have flung themselves into revolutionary action with the almost physiological brutality that centuries of oppression give rise to and feed.[21]

As Fanon recounts, the nationalist leaders hesitated to use tactics on human and political grounds. They abandoned plans of terrorism on some occasions or even in the last minute called off the *fidai*[22] entrusted with planting a given bomb. The killing and wounding of civilians brought agonizing memories. On political grounds, the nationalist leaders wanted to avoid whatever might alienate people from the cause of independence and freedom, such as, the French democrats, and democrats all over the world, and particularly the Europeans of Algeria who supported the Algerian independence.[23]

However, terror tactics were adopted by FLN as a counter measure against the terrorism which put French territorial units at advantage. It was directed against members of the police, meeting places like cafes. Since the members of the police and the army were the arms of the oppressive system, and were shooting and killing some members of the FLN and supporters, Fanon could argue for the violence against them on the principle of self-defense reinforced by the principle of double effect. In shooting at the members of the police and at the soldiers in skirmishes, the revolutionary fighters on the part of the colonized or oppressed may not be intending the death of the members of the police and of the soldiers, which is the evil effect of their self-defensive action but only the good effect of restraining the violence and oppression of the police and the soldiers, and thereby protect their own lives and values and those of their fellow natives. Here the same action or performance of the defending native soldiers or revolutionaries gives rise to two effects, namely, the good effect which is intended and the evil effect which is not intended but only allowed. The cause is proportionately grave in that what is at stake is human lives and values, and nonviolent means have been tried by the natives to gain freedom and have been opposed by violence by the French authorites.

However, I think that Fanon is against terrorism directed against the innocent, and against the self-defensive force of the oppressed denegrating into revengeful episodes and arbitrary violence. His battle of conscience on these issues can be felt even in the turmoil of *The Wretched of the Earth*, which is heavily colored with violence. Self-defensive violence has a limited use. His revolutionary violence avoids feeding on mere vindictiveness. It is violence that would not be used if the natives were not pressed to the wall. On this he writes:

> Racial feeling, as opposed to racial prejudice, and that determination to fight for one's life which characterizes the native's reply to oppression are obviously good enough reasons for joining the fight. But you do not carry on a war, nor suffer brutal and widespread oppression, nor look on while all other members of your family are wiped out in order to make racialism or hatred triumph. Racialism and hatred and resentment—"a legitimate desire for revenge"—cannot sustain a war of liberation. Those lightning flashes of consciousness which fling the boy into stormy paths or which throw him into an almost pathological trance where the face of the other beckons one to giddiness, where my blood calls for the blood of the other, where by sheer inertia my death calls for the death of the other —that intense emotion of the first few hours falls to pieces if it is left to feed on its own substance ... You'll never overthrow the terrible enemy machine and you won't change human beings, if you forget to raise the standard of consciousness of the rank and file.[24]

The above passage shows how the use of violence to effect social and political changes must not be artibrary, but rather must be dicated by the desire for authentic humanism; for, as Fanon maintains, the basic motivation is to change man for the better by raising "the standard of consciousness of the rank-and-file," because men have a claim on their fellowmen to receive decent treatment. Although this is hard to accomplish in a war of liberation, it is a basic principle of action, because, according to Fanon, action should help man to humanize the world by preserving his respect for the basic values that constitute the human world; and it can end up in "incoherent agitation if it does not serve to reconstruct the consciousness of the individual."

Consequently, I think that to take up arms is the last resort, Fanon would agree, because revolutionary violence is a costly weapon in its ambivalence. Unqualified commitment to violence is alien to genuine humanism. A revolutionary must, therefore, be responsible in taking the first step and continued steps in a revolution. Fanon attempts to do so as he agonized over the debris of revolutionary violence. To him, revolutionary violence as a self-defensive means has strictly limited use in view of his theory of praxis (action). The problem with revolutionary violence, as I have already pointed out, is that it is more often excessive in the hand of those who are fighting for freedom, since there is the danger of freedom degenerating into license in a spirit of revenge. Fanon warns against this.

The above discussion shows how false is the picture painted of Fanon as a rabid revolutionary without redeeming features because he advocates violence. We have attempted to distinguish the various aspects of his espousal of violence. The context of his writing has to be taken into account if one wants to do justice to his attitude to revolutionary violence. The colonial world, particularly the French Colonial System in Algeria, as he saw it, was ridden with violence, and so liberation would involve violent confrontation where power corrupted, and was not amenable to rational persuasion to grant freedom to the colonized.

As we have already indicated, Fanon operates within a dialectical framework in which the principle of self-defense reinforced by the principle of double effect operates in the achievement of the reconciliation between humanism and violence. In a certain sense, within his dialectical framework his humanism is reconciled with violence in a dialectical tension. This requires some explanation.

To Fanon, as we have seen, the liberation movement or revolution is a dialectical process. As an interpretor of the colonial system, he sees the historical process of the colonial system as a dialectical process with the seeds of its own destruction sown[25] when violence was used by the colonial power and colonizers to pacify the natives. Where violence is used to "keep the peace," the "peace" can only endure as long as force and violence are operative, and will cease when the oppressed have the power to throw off the yoke. Here force calls for force.

As Fanon puts it:

> The colonia situation is first of all a military conquest continued and reinforced by civil and police administration. In Algeria, as in every colony, the foreign oppressor looks upon the native as marking a limit to his dignity and defines himself as constituting an irreducible negation of the colonized country's national existence.[20]

To comment, the colonizer, by defining his status as a negation of the independence of the colonized, sows the seed of the self-defensive force on the part of the colonized, which will eventually bring about the destruction of his own status. Fanon agrees with M. Martin Chauffie's report that the colonial system corrupts those who become an instrument of sadistic perversion.[27] The raping and murdering of Algerian girls and women make a grisly reading. When power corrupts, it expresses itself in contradictions as it attempts to perpetuate itself. It becomes a prisoner of its own domination. On this point Fanon writes about the French colonial power in Algeria:

> Because for 130 years the French national consciousness has been conditioned by one simple basic principle—Algeria *is* French—we today find ourselves up against instinctive, passionate, anti-historic reactions, at a moment when a large proportion of the French people rationally realize that its interest can best be served by putting an end to the war and recognizing an independent Algerian State.

> Never was the principle according to which no one can enslave another so wholly true. After having domesticated the Algerian people for more than a century, France finds herself a prisoner of her conquest and incapable of detaching herself from it, of defining new relations, of making a fresh start.[28]

By way of commentary, we could say that the French colonial power, by trying to maintain itself by all forms of violence against the aspirations of the natives to freedom, acts in contradiction to the French people's appreciation of freedom for which the French people had often fought.

Fanon calls on the French people to rid itself of this basic contradiction of the colonial mentality:

> The Algerian people's fight is a radical criticism of the pseudo-right of the property (*our* Africa south of the Sahara, *our* Algeria) and at the same time a challenge to the French people to criticize itself, to rid itself of the colonialist, anti-democratic and racist mentality, in short, to live and go beyond the historical-

ly elaborated contradictions.

The decisive and implacable criticism of Senator (John F.) Kennedy, the fundamentally anti-colonialist positions adopted by the British Laborites and, more generally, the recent position adopted by the American official services, reveal two phenomena. In the first place, the historic and general process of liberation of colonial peoples is recognized, identified, and accepted; also the certainty has been acquired, after analysis, that the Algerian people has put its whole weight behind the struggle and that it is really hard to see how France could fail to recognize Algeria's independence.[29]

The above quotation shows how the need to go beyond the contradictions of the colonial system is recognized by men of good will and how Fanon's confidence in the success of the Algerian revolution is not merely utopian. Unfortunately, France intensified its military effort to keep down the natives of her Algerian colony. Fanon believes that by so doing the French people has imposed on the Algerian people immense sacrifices which would not be unavailing.[30] The blood of the Algerians would not flow in vain.

Fanon's revolutionary humanism works against the colonial system and beyond. According to him, the colonial situation is opposed to universal humanism, and brings into being two "species" of men,[31] namely, the colonizer and the colonized. Man is colonizer and man as colonized (oppressed) are internally opposed,[32] and must be replaced by the "new man" of the "new humanism" (universal humanism), because "to fight for the humanization of repression is futile."[33] This is what he means by saying that the slavery of man by man must end forever. In view of the dialectical framework, the thesis of the superiority complex of the colonizer and the inferiority complex of the colonized calls for opposition by force on the part of the colonized in the effort to assert their human dignity and value. From his adoption of Hegel's dynamic concept of man we have seen how Fanon prizes struggle for recognition and freedom as an aspect of being human: the ability to negate whatever dehumanizes and destroys freedom is an essential aspect of being human.

Consequently, self-defensive violence on the part of the colonized or oppressed becomes a necessary dialectical response to the thesis of the colonial subjugation and occupation. Since power recognizes power, the self-defensive power of the colonized or oppressed makes it possible for the colonizer or oppressor to change his stance of superiority in terms of power, and accord recognition to the colonized or oppressed. Thus the position of man as colonizer or oppressor is transcended by the stage of mutual recognition. By bringing about the liberation of the colonized, the first step toward universal humanism, violence plays a mediating role in the resolution of the colonial contradictions. Fanon, as we have seen, is sensitive to the evil effects of violence, such as, the killings and destruction of war of liberation. I would agree therefore that Fanon would intend the good effects of liberating the colonized or oppressed, and not intend the evil effects of violence in view of establishing universal humanism. Hence, at this level within his dialectical framework, humanism and violence are reconciled but not without some tension between them.

Furthermore, the fact that Fanon discountenances arbitrary violence and violence of revenge shows how delicate the reconciliation and tension between humanism and violence are in him. He projects that the colonized or oppressed win cleanly; that is, without the debris of violence in the form of tolls in human lives and destruction of property. However, he espouses violence as the last resort where the colonizer is determined to suppress the humanity of the colonized. Hence violence is poised within the mitigating circumstance of self-defense on the part of the colonized or oppressed. It is a necessary evil that must be deplored. Since the ability to defend oneself with an appropriately effective force which may result in injury or death where there is a challenge to one's humanity is truly to be human, there is a tension between this and the spirit of reconciliation, love and peace which Fanon advocates. Consequently, Fanon does not achieve a completely neat reconciliation between his espousal of violence and his humanism. Violence is always something to be deplored even though it can be justified in self-defense, because, as Fanon believes, we must change our ways, invent, and work out new concepts toward genuine humanism which has love, communication, mutual recognition as the binding force.

Since the colonial situation constitutes a negation of the basic human vlaues of recognition and freedom, its replacement is a need of the first order. There can be no love and peace among men where the human is denied to others. This is the point of Fanon's revolutionary humanism. Thus he puts it:

We Africans say that the problem of peace among men—non-African, in the present instance—is fundamental, but we also say that the liberation of Africa, of the last bastions of colonialism, constitutes the first problem.[34]

The alternative to violence is to abandon the use of violence, and use only moral persuasion. What happens when this fails to change the situation? Pacificism as an alternative in a colonial system where power wants to maintain its own by power does not seem to be morally effective,[35] although nonviolence as a means of settling human conflicts remains the ideal. Fanon recognizes this point.

In his espousal of violence, Fanon reveals the tension of a man grappling with the problem of a complex situation, and not a man who has no qualms in the use of violence as he has been portrayed by many writers. By prizing struggle in the defense of one's right to human dignity, he believes that it would be inhuman for the oppressed to take things lying down. Hence revolutionary humanism is an authentic way of asserting the humanity of the oppressed. It becomes the expression of the power of the negative in man to say "no" to whatever dehumanizes by taking appropriate measures to forestall and terminate the condition of alienation. As the oppressors' values or alleged values are affirmed by violence, so the natives or the oppressed react by reaffirming or by defending their rights and values which have been devalued. The native has been bound with myths which show him up as an inferior species. Fanon contends that in the liberation struggle he gives a lie to the value-judgmental picture made of him. This constitutes the basis of the emergence of the new man on the part of the oppressed.

Hence, the spirit of reconciliation of Fanon's humanism is based first and foremost on the recognition of the humanity of the oppressed or colonized or of all men. Since violence here is placed at the level of self-defense reinforced by the principle of double effect on the part of the colonized, its mediating role in the first step of reconciliation where the humanity of the oppressed is denied, is not in principle opposed to a project of an authentically universalist humanism. The cathartic or therapeutic function of violence which Fanon holds can be seen in self-defensive violence as the oppressed repudiate their inferiority complex and assert their humanity, and not in arbitrary violence.

On the other hand, those who regard Fanon as an apostle of violence, who considers violence to be good in itself, either ignore or are unaware of the context of self-defense when they quote the following key passages:

> Violence is . . . seen as comparable to a royal pardon. The colonized man finds his freedom in and through violence.[36] But it so happens that for the colonized people this violence, because it constitutes their only work, invests their characters with positive and creative qualities. The practice of violence binds them together as a whole, since each individual forms a violent link in the great chain, a part of the great organism of violence which has surged upward in reaction to the settlers' violence in the beginning. The groups recognize each other and the future nation is already indivisible. The armed struggle mobilizes the people; that is to say, it throws them in one way and in one direction.[37]

> At the level of individuals, violence is a cleansing force. It frees the native from his inferiority complex and from despair and inaction; it makes him fearless and restores his self-respect.[38]

However, a careful reading of these passages in context shows that they are located within the context of self-defense. In the first place, they are set against the background of the colonial world where the colonized natives reach "a point of no return" in their determination to oppose their dehumanization by the colonialists.[39] Secondly, the colonial world is described by Fanon as Manichean: "On the logical plane, the Manicheism of the settler produces a Manicheism of the native;"[40] and the alleged "absolute evil of the native" confronts the "absolute evil of the settler." The "evil" of the settler is violence in the form of dehumanizing the natives, killing and torturing. Reflecting on the ambivalence of the course of armed liberation (violence) taken by the natives, Fanon, instead of praising it, describes it as "apparent folly," "spiritual aberration" because it springs from the "intuition of the colonized masses" that their liberation must, and can only, be achieved by force." Here one should note that Fanon criticizes spontaneity for its weakness. The uncertainty of an effective use of violence on the part of the natives makes violence "a disgraceful thing,"[41] when it pervades a political party. As I have indicated, violence is a "necessary evil" from which positive or therapeutic effects such as self-respect, liberation and freedom arise on the part of the natives. Hence, Fanon does not regard violence as a good in itself. Although he espouses revolutionary violence for the above mentioned effects, he deplores it as a means which would not have been used if the natives had an alternative. But violence interpreted as "uncompromising action," that is, the determination of the natives to oppose all forms of exploitation and degradation is a "good" in a qualified sense because it raises their morale.

We may remark here that there is a dialectical progression in Fanon's revolutionary humanism as the overcoming of the colonial situation is dialectically connected with the liberation of all the wretched of the earch, that is, with the liberation of man. Fanon expresses this point as follows:

> The dialectical strengthening that occurs between the movement of liberation of the colonized peoples and the emancipatory struggle of the working classes of the imperialist countries is sometimes neglected, and indeed forgotten.

> The process of liberation of man, independently of the concrete situations in which he finds himself, includes and concerns the whole of humanity. The fight for national dignity gives its true meaning to the struggle for bread and social dignity. This internal relation is one of the roots of the immense solidarity that unites the oppressed peoples to the exploited masses of the colonialist countries.[42]

Although Fanon does not work out in detail the dialectical progression[43] of his revolutionary humanism, we have attempted to show that it begins from the resolution of the contradictions of the colonial system through the mediation of violence considered on the principle of self-defense, which is reinforced by the principle of double effect, then to the liberation of the colonized, and then to the wretched of the earth, and finally to the stage of universal recognition of the dignity and freedom of all men and women.

We may also remark here that an important insight from our investigation of Fanon's revolutionary humanism with regard to the use of violence is that in Fanon the dialectic does not freewheel with material conditions as in Marx, but takes into account the moral values. This is why the reconciliation of his humanism with his espousal of violence on the principle of self-defense supported by the principle of double effect is in place.

Chapter VI
AFRICA AND THE WORLD

Africa has, relatively speaking, remained the "Dark-Continent" to those who do not know its rich and diverse cultural traditions. But Africa has, in fact, been known from the dawn of man's history, from the times of the Pharaohs of Egypt, the emperors of Ethiopia, in the periods of ancient kingdoms of Ghana, Biafra and Benin. The cry of a Roman proconsul, *"Semper novi quid ex Africa,"* expresses the fascination of Africa in the ancient world. It is regrettable that the rich traditions and wealth of Africa have long been submerged by the veneer of colonialism. Today the cultural richness and wealth of Africa are now being brought to light by unabiased excavations of paleontologists and by investigations of anthropologists, historians, and philologists. The "sleeping giant" is now taking its rightful place among the great continents of the world.

The thrust of Fanon's revolutionary humanism, as one can see from the preceding chapters, is, to a large extent, to bring real Africa to light. The decolonization of Algeria is but the thin edge of the wedge to total liberation of Africa. Fanon recognizes the cultural richness and potential wealth of Africa; but they are not static in the wake of decolonization. From the existentialist point of view, decolonization expresses the evolution of African cultures in the light of his "new humanism."

One may ask whether Fanon, by projecting the Algerian revolution as a model for all of Africa, does not ignore the diversity and differences in "the Great Giant." Africa was colonized by different European powers which adopted different attitudes and policies. It is not fair to lump them all together without, at least, recognizing their differences. Some of them kept to the principle of force and violence to the end in order to maintain their "right;" and some tried to grant in-dependence gradually without convulsive revolutions. Fanon, however, advocates radical revolution because colonization, in a certain sense, was thorough, and nothing short of radically uncompromising action would reinstate the people's appre-ciation of their humanity.

Fanon's tendency to generalization is his strength, and at times his weakness. He adopts Karl Jaspers' principle which states that "comprehension in depth of a single in-stance will often enable us, phenomenologically to apply this understanding in general to innumerable cases. Often what one has once grasped is soon met again. What is im-portant in phenomenology is less the study of a large number of instances than the intuitive and deep understanding of a few individual cases."[1] This means that the universal is embodied in the particular. It is important to point out here that the danger of this kind of generalization is to overlook the differences between the given case or cases and others at large. Fanon often emphasizes the similarities of Black con-sciousness, for example, to the point that the differences in the colonized self of the different Black groups do not re-ceive adequate emphasis. The Antilean Negro or American Negro is different from the African Negro if only because of background. The Black consciousness which has been enslaved is different from that which has not been, and their re-spective attitudes to the White consciousness may be dif-ferent. One might suggest that Fanon wants to stress the inherent evil of racism and colonialism, which is deper-sonalization. These are two faces of the same coin, and their effects are corrosive in any case.

Since philosophical reflection is, to a great extent, an effort to clarify or discover the essential principles underlying exper-ience and what ought to be as a standard to judge what is the case, Fanon from the philosophical standpoint, reflects on Black and White experiences in racism and colonialism in order to point out how racism and colonialism distort the human dimension of these consciousnesses. Here Fanon's method, as David Caute points out is "to fuse the descriptive and the norma-tive, to put the 'like it is' at the service of the 'like it ought to be.' "[2] Fanon describes and analyses Black experience, and pro-jects the remedy for the Black problem. By avoiding the merely subjective in his description of the Black situation, he reveals the innately human desire for the universal. He had to wrestle with the problem of man in the particular and in the general.

The Black problem can only be understood and solved as a facet of the human problem.

1. AFRICAN UNITY

Despite cultural differences in the African landscape, Fanon was a strong advocate of African unity in the form of Pan-Africanism.[3] Pan-Africanism was a movement spearheaded by some leaders of African descent and Africans after the First World War to reconstruct Africa for Africans and humanity.

Under the able leadership of Mr. M. Blaise Diagne and Dr. W.E. Burghardt Du Bois,[4] the first Pan-African Congress was organized in February 19, 20, 21, 1919 at the Grand Hotel Boulevard des Capucines, Paris. Among the items discussed were the ideal of racial unity of all of African descent and racial equality, the maintenance of human rights irrespective of colour, race and sex in the world at large, and decolonization of Africa in the interest of justice and humanity. Resolutions were made with regard to realizing these in practice.

Fanon has been called "a Pan-African revisionist."[5] He envisaged the evolution of a united front on the part of Africans against colonialism and neo-colonialism. Unity gives a great measure of strength; but individualism and divisiveness which colonial policies encouraged tend to achieve little; hence one can see the prescriptive stance of the ideal of unity and universalism in his humanism.

However, Fanon's enthusiasm "to put Africa in motion, to cooperate in its organization, in its regrouping behind revolutionary principles"[6] has met with mixed reception from critics. His humanistic picture of Africa is a blend of realism and idealism:

> The Africa of everyday, oh not the poets' Africa, the one that puts to sleep, but the one that prevents sleep, for the people is impatient to do, to play, to say. The people that says: "I want to build, to love, to respect, to create."[7]

His vision of Pan Africanism is based on this picture of Africa. It sounds utopian[8]. However, Fanon is not merely describing the *de facto* situation, but is projecting a revolution in sensitivity and in the ordering of values. The "ought" is to be laid against the "is" as a measure. There is no praxis which inherently determines consciousness without the ideal. The ideal makes the real possible. African personality can only emerge from the unity of Africa despite differences.[9]

In his effort to refurbish the idea of Pan Africanism, he attended the All-African People's Congress which was held in Accra, Ghana in December, 1958. At this conference he passionately spoke about the Algerian people's struggle in order to enlist the support of African nationalist leaders. He is said to have stopped suddenly in the middle of his speech because he was overcome with emotion as he visualized the carnage in the Algerian struggle.[10] Present at the conference were Kwame Nkrumah of Ghana, Patrice Lumumba of Congo (now Zaire), Felix Moumie of the Cameroons, Tom Mboya of Kenya, and Holden Roberto of Angola. He urged the nationalist leaders of newly independent nations and those still under the colonial yoke to support one another in a concerted effort to bring a new Africa to birth. He envisaged the emergence of a creative unity of the North and South of Africa.

His rounds took him to the Second Congress of Black Writers in Rome, March 1959, to the Second Conference of African Peoples in Tunis, January 1960, to Positive Action Conference for Peace and Security in Africa, to the Afro-Asian Solidarity Conference in Conakry, Guinea, and to the Third Conference of Independent African States at Addis-Ababa, June 1960.

Appointed the representative of the Algerian Provisional Government in March 1960, Fanon devoted attention to establishing a center in Mali[11] for recruiting soldiers and getting arms for the Algerian war, and for events taking place in Congo and Angola. He also saw to the establishment of a Pan African army for decolonizing the continent. He faced many risks as he became deeply involved in the anti-colonial revolutionary establishment. Marked out for assassination by French Secret Agents, he escaped being killed as his car was blown up on an Algerian-Moroccan mission. Two attempts were made on his life in Rome. In 1960 attempts were made to capture him during his mission at Accra, Ghana. But he managed to elude the grasp of his enemies. He might have thought that the liberation of Africa was worth the risks.

Fanon levelled scathing criticism on advocates of "Franco-African Unity," which he thought was the colonial relation of the French Union in a new guise. This is disruptive of the African personality. Underpinning Fanon's criticism is the principle of equality among peoples and cultures. In this vein, he advocated a complete break from the colonial past in view of forging the unity of a new Africa which can be destroyed by the forces of neo-colonialism.

Fanon has been criticized for advocating a complete break from Europe, but such criticism would be unjustified if his concern for African integrity on the human level is not taken into account: colonialist and neo-colonist attitudes and arrangements stultify real independence and freedom of Africa. Any relationship tinged with colonialist mentality is always dehumanizing. Only interaction and communication on the basis of equal respect among nations and peoples make for genuine humanism. However, I think that Fanon was overreacting in advocating complete break with Europe in view of the fact that he also advocates economic and technical aid from Europe to developing countries in the Third World.[12]

It is regrettable that the unity of Africa has not been firmly and completely established, and that the measure of unity attained so far is threatened today by conflicts among some newly independent nations of Africa. These conflicts have taken the form of border disputes which have given rise to wars. The history of some of the newly independent nations of Africa has been marred by a spate of internal conflicts and civil wars, which have offered the former colonial powers excuse to intervene. Fanon distrusted the intervention of the United Nations in trying to resolve these conflicts.

2. REPARATION FOR COLONIAL INJUSTICE

Africa, Fanon thinks, should be given redress for colonial exploitation.[13] Africa has been fleeced to clothe Europe; and despoiled, it limps under the despicable gaze of the colonialist. Raw materials were cheaply taken from Africa to feed the factories in Europe. Slave labour from the colonies built up Europe. Economic crisis in the colonialist country often found resolution in the economic and political exploitation of the colonized country. Neither human nor international justice was given a chance to operate in the colonial system. Hence, as Fanon believed, the colonialist worker's interest is antithetical to the interest of the colonized. "The struggle against colonialism, in its specific aspects of exploitation of man by man, thus belongs in the general process of man's liberation."[14]

Fanon calls for the abandonment of the unethical principle that "might is right" on which colonialism is founded, and for the return of politics to the moral domain; for the human is moral. It is empty to talk of peace, communication and interaction among races and peoples without doing something to eliminate injustice, exploitation and racism. Peace is built

99

on justice and mutual recognition of the human dignity of others. The dominance of one race or people throws the human order out of balance. Hence, reparation to Africa with regard to decolonization, granting of independence and economic support is in order. Economic aid to Africa is not charity; it is more of a demand of justice.

Fanon calls on the Big Powers to diffuse the mounting tensions which result from nuclear armament and cold war, and to reorder their priorities for ameliorating the condition of mankind by just distribution of the wealth of the earth. He writes:

> We ought . . . to emphasize and explain to the capitalist countries that the fundamental problems of our time is not the struggle between the socialist regime and them. The Cold War must be ended, for it leads nowhere. The plans for nuclearizing the war must stop, and large scale investment and technical aid must be given to the underdeveloped regions. The fate of the world depends on the answer that is given to this question.[16]

Fanon's insight is that Africa should not try to become Europe, but must try to mediate in the polarization of the East and West in their ideologies, and not add to the flames. Because "if we want humanity to advance a step further, if we want to bring it up to a different level than that which Europe has shown it, then we must invent and we must make discoveries."[15] Although Fanon was a little too far in his criticism of Europe, he has a good point in view of colonial and world war experiences which mar its humanism. The world needs a better example to follow. At best, European humanism had a limited vision which has to be transcended in the historical process. It did not envision the universalist humanism which includes all humanity.

Chapter VII
REVOLUTIONARY PRAXIS

One of the most important aspects of Fanon's revolutionary humanism is that it is praxis. Here he adopts Marx's concept of praxis to his vision of socio-political change. Marx wrote:

> The philosophers have only *interpreted* the world in various ways; the point, however, is to change it.[1]

Marx maintains that praxis is a correlate of theory, that knowledge or ideas to be meaningful must be translated into action. In other words, ideas must be employed in ameliorating social conditions, in rectifying economic imbalance, and thereby remove the condition of alienation.

According to Marx, human praxis is realized in man's dialectical relation with nature, in economic relations and forces. For instance, he defines the social class by the group's position in the productive process. He thought that the proletarian revolution would inevitably follow from the autonomy of economic development. But he was mistaken in his calculation because the revolution did not produce corresponding social conditions. Following Jean Paul Sartre in the tradition of existentialist defense of freedom, but unlike Marx, Fanon, as we have indicated before, believed in man using his freedom to intervene in the praxis of revolution. Revolutionary change which brings a new order of values and expectations is the intentional act of those who spearhead a revolution. Oppressed peoples have a free role to play in their liberation.

Since human action is the expression of human thought and freedom, a corresponding theory of praxis must bear the stamp of amenability to change in view of activity and experience. Geisman sees this as the source of the contradictions in Fanon's writings.[2] I think that it would be wrong to push the "contradictions" in Fanon's writing too far in view of his universalist humanism. As I have endeavoured to show in chapter V, the contradictions are more apparent than real. Fanon may have revised his theory of action but not to the extent of contradicting the ultimate vision of his humanism.

With an existentialist base in his philosophy of action, Fanon maintains man's self-creativity in praxis as he upholds Sartre's existentialist thesis that existence precedes essence.[3] Hence action is not a random event but a creation of a human order and values which are superior to what actually exists. Through action man should humanize the world. Revolutionary humanism is essentially a human praxis whereby authentic human order and values are initially forged. It restores the imbalance of one race or people dominating another. Specifically, it is a criticism of the White world inferiorizing and exploiting the Black world, of the European settlers in Algeria dominating the Moslems, slave labour being used for the aggrandisement of Europe. It is a practical way of rectifying the injustices perpetuated in the relationship of the colonial powers of the west and the "Third World" (a term which should be replaced by "Developing Nations" because "Third World" carries a negative connotation of a relation of superiority and inferiority).

Here Fanon disagrees with Hegel's dialectical interpretation of history which concerns the past. To Hegel, the philosopher stands outside the stage of the dialectical development of the historical process, contemplates and describes it. One can see that it is not difficult to understand Hegel's criterion of justifying a revolution, viz., its success; if it fails, it is not justified. But for Fanon, the problem is to justify it before it occurs. Action is required for putting things right in the present and future. The power of negative thinking must be translated into action. Truth is in action. Fanon considers the fellah who joins in the liberation movement as possessing the truth. The moment of rebellion is the moment of asserting existence and self-creation on the individual and national levels. There is no indifference to what is going on on the part of the oppressed and all men of men of good will; for as Carmichael said: "If you are not a part of the solution, you are a part of the problem." It is the participant, by way of activity, who writes a revolutionary song.

REVOLUTIONARY AGENCIES

As we have already seen, Fanon adapts Marx's theory to the

colonial system, the "Third World" with reference to praxis in socio-political revolution. Marx identifies the bourgeoisie and the proletariat as the chief protagonists in socio-political revolution in the industrialized society of the West.

Reflecting on the written history of Western Europe, Marx sees it as a history of class conflict, which has eventuated in the conflict of these two classes. He eulogizes the bourgeoisie for playing a "most revolutionary role in history;"[4] and contends that the bourgeoisie, the modern capitalist class, has brought about the disintegration of the feudal system by revolutionizing instruments of production, which affect production relations, and change the gamut of social relations. Its enterprising spirit has made it a world power of the means of production and exchange in modern industry, of exploiting raw materials and world markets.[5]

However, Marx criticizes the bourgeois class for losing its revolutionary edge by becoming conservative, because it consolidates its gains in capitalistic system which alienates the proletariat, the working class. The proletariat then becomes the dialectical opposite of the bourgeoisie; and he identifies the former as the revolutionary class in the contemporary world.[6]

The proletariat is defined by Marx with reference to having marketable labour which is exploited by the bourgeoisie which owns the means of production. The proletarians are the wretched of the earth, who "have nothing to lose but their chain" in the revolution whereby capital is wrestled out of the hand of the capitalists and communalized in the temporary dictatorship of the proletariat, because capital is considered by Marx as the source of exploitation and alienation of the worker. The proletarian revolution would eventually bring about a classless society where man would no longer be exploited by another.

But in the colonial system there are no classes in the strictly Marxian sense, because the colonial system is not industrialized. Accordingly, there are parallels by approximation. Hence Fanon sees the following four main social classes: the national bourgeoisie, the urban-proletariat, the peasants, and the lumpen-proletariat. As Emmanual Hansen has pointed out, "he does not define his social classes in any precise terms, he characterizes them in such a way as to make them easily identifiable."[7] Among the "social classes" he highlights the revolutionary role of the lumpen-proletariat, unlike Marx who stresses the role of the proletariat.

Fanon characterizes the national bourgeoisie as follows:

a sort of little greedy caste, avid and voracious, with the mind of a huckster, only too glad to accept the dividends that the former colonial power hands out to it. This get-rich-quick middle class shows itself incapable of great ideas or of inventiveness. It remembers what it has read in European textbooks and imperceptibly it becomes not even the replica of Europe, but its caricature.[8]

Constituting the "middle class," the national bourgeoisie of the developing nations are men of the liberal professions such as lawyers, teachers, doctors, administrators and business men. Unlike their European counterpart which has economic power by consolidating capital and are dynamic, they lack economic and productive power. It is rather "the tool of capitalism."[9] It lacks the force of character that could make it play a relevant role in the revolutionary decolonization, because it is profiting from the colonial regime. It wants to take over the former privileges of the colonial masters. To join in the revolutionary decolonization, the national bourgeoisie ought to repudiate its role as "a tool of capitalism" and "make itself the willing slave of that revolutionary capital which is the people."[10]

The urban proletariat consists of the working class which keeps the colonial machine running. This class "includes train conductors, taxi drivers, miners, dockers, interpreters, nurses, and so on."[11] Fanon does not consider this class as strongly revolutionary because of their "privileged place" in the colonial system. They are a part of the "bourgeoisie" among the colonized people. It follows the nationalist party line.

The peasants are the class of country people who cultivate the land. Big farmers should be distinguished from the general mass of the peasantry. It is debatable whether Fanon regards the country people as an undifferentiated mass. Emmanuel Hansen is right in arguing that Fanon distinguishes the peasantry as such and the rich farmers.[12]

The peasants, Fanon maintains, have the most revolutionary potentials in decolonization. They constitute the most revolutionary force, because they have maintained their society and traditions and are distrustful of the colonial power and its beneficiaries, such as the townsmen. Rather than gain from the colonial system, they have been exploited. Fanon writes:

The peasant who stays put defends his traditions stubbornly, and in a colonized society stands for the disciplined element whose interests lie in maintaining the social structure. It is true that this unchanging way of life, which hangs on like grim death to rigid social structures, may occasionally give birth to movements which are based on religious fanaticism or tribal wars. But in their spontaneous movements the country people as a whole remain disciplined and altruistic. The individual stands aside in favor of the community.[13]

Fanon regrets the fact that the peasants have generally been excluded from the mainstream of politics by the emergent native political parties. Their virtues of discipline and altruism are essential in the struggle for national liberation. Their spontaneous revolts against the colonial system should be supported and channeled towards the national liberation.

The lumpen-proletariat is a subclass of the peasantry, which constitutes the revolutionary core in the struggle for national liberation. They are peasants who have been uprooted from the country districts as a result of colonial expropriation and exploitation. Being landless, they move into the towns to look for jobs in ports and cities. Fanon identifies them as "that horde of starving men uprooted from their tribes and from their clan."[14] In a characteristic metaphor, he describes them for their doggedness as "a horde of rats; you may kick them and throw stones at them, but despite your efforts they'll go on gnawing at the roots of the tree."[15] Specifically, this class includes "the pimps, the hooligans, the unemployed, and petty criminals . . . prostitutes . . . all the hopeless class of humanity."[16] The lumpen-proletariat qualify as the revolutionary force, because they are the truly disinherited mass of humanity which have not profited from the colonial system; and like the Marxian proletariat they have nothing to lose, and have everything to gain in the national liberation. This class refuses to reform in order to be in line with the colonial establishment. It uses violence spontaneously.

However, the lumpen-proletariat, Fanon cautions, has the weakness of "ignorance and incomprehension" which colonial agents could turn to good account in the ambiguity of the colonial situation if care is not taken. For example, they could be hired to fight or be of help on the side of the colonial troops.[17] Their spontaneity in the use of violence which makes them eminently revolutionary is ambivalent in that it could be a source of strength or weakness. They need political education and organization in order to avoid the pitfalls of spontaneity. By their spontaneous uprising in the outskirts of the suburbs where they infiltrate, they constitute a danger to the "security" of the colonial towns.

One wonders whether Fanon is altogether right in making

the peasantry[18] the revolutionary front instead of the rising class of civil servants and party members in the emerging nations. The lumpen-proletariat and the rest of the peasantry may not be equal to the task of revolutionary action in overthrowing the colonial forces if the middle class fails to participate. Fanon distrusted the latter, as we have seen, because he thought they had profited and are profiting from the colonial system and the neo-colonialism which was stalking the land. They were, therefore, unable to take radical and uncompromising action. So they edged with compromises which Fanon disavowed. One may argue that Fanon was not right here, for compromise may be a way of finding political identity out of the native and colonial heritage. It takes time, patience, hard work, and resources to build a nation.

Fanon's eulogy of the peasantry as the revolutionary agency in decolonization is tinged with exaggeration. Of all the members of the colonial world Fanon maintains that the peasants live in close societal bond and are not alienated from their culture. One may ask, if they are not alienated, how is it that they are in the forefront of revolution which is the theatre for the alienated? Generally the less a person is alienated, the less he is a revolutionary potential. As Emmanuel Hansen points out from the sociological point of view: "Innovations are nearly always caused by marginal men. The integrated always have reasons to explain their adverse conditions: it is the will of the gods, or some other fatalistic reason; but the alienated is more likely to blame either himself or the one he thinks responsible for his condition, and to do something about it."[19] The solution to this problem in Fanon may be seen in his conflating the lumpen-proletariat which are alienated with the rest of the peasantry whose alienation as a result of colonial exploitation is minimized by its attachment to its traditional values.

As Hansen also points out, there is a contradiction in saying at the same time that the peasants are "rebels by instinct" and are also the "most disciplined." Maybe Fanon is stating the untamed aggressiveness in human nature to self-defense on the part of the peasants and the discipline which results from political education. They are more easily led than the intellectual type.

Fanon has also been taken to task for maintaining that the peasants are "spontaneously revolutionary." Nguyen Nghe[20] and Marina Ottawa[21] argue against Fanon by maintaining that the peasants can only become revolutionary when conscientized and that they often fall back to old ways after independence without carrying out the necessary structural changes.

As I have said before, Fanon appears to overstate the revolutionary potentials of the peasants. However, this has to be balanced with Fanon's insistence that they need political education from the intellectuals who are involved in the revolution. Fanon writes:

> To hold a responsible position in an underdeveloped country is to know that in the end everything depends on the education of the masses, on the raising of the level of thought, and on what we are too quick to call "political teaching."

> . . . Now, political education means opening their minds, awakening them, and allowing the birth of their intelligence; as Cesaire said it is "to invent souls." To educate the masses politically does not mean, cannot mean, making a political speech. What it means is to try, relentlessly and passionately, to teach the masses that everything depends on them; that if we stagnate it is their responsibility, and that if we go forward it is due to them too, that there is no such thing as a demiurge, that there is no famous man who will take responsibility for everything, but that the demiurge is the people themselves and magic hands are finally only the hands of the people.[22]

Although revolution can spark off with the revolt of the peasants (lumpen-proletariat), it needs to be sustained by political education in view of genuine humanism. The peasants play a critical role in the national struggle. Colonial revolution is the people's war. Fanon, like Marx, advocates socio-political revolution and not merely a political one. Hence, the involvement of the masses, in the case of Marx, the proletariat, and in the case of Fanon, the peasants (lumpen-proletariat included).

The social truth in the dialectics of genuine revolutionary humanism which Fanon presupposed is that when all share in making sacrifice for national liberation all should share in reaping its fruit. This expectation often evaporates in the light of experience, when the party platform becomes an empty sounding board for the personal aggrandizement of the members as they try to consolidate their position by dictatorship, and not for the good of the people. This is tantamount to a betrayal of the cause for which the people struggled. Warring factions and a spate of army coups in a struggle for power undo the common good that liberation ushers in. These threatened Algeria and continue to threaten other parts of Africa.[23]

Chapter VIII
SOCIO-POLITICAL IDEAL

The aim of revolutionary humanism is to destroy alienating socio-political structures and replace them with ideal structures or approximations which offer opportunities for the full development of human beings. In the former, the instrumentality of violence is evident, but in the latter, Fanon's feeling for nonviolence in human relationships begins to come into focus. Colonial revolution is a stage toward establishing authentic humanism where non-violence should dominate. For Fanon did not want to be a professional revolutionary.[1]

1. CRITICISM OF NATIONALIST PARTIES

Fanon prefaced his vision of an ideal socio-political structure in the developing nations after independence with a criticism of nationalist parties which emerged to take over the reins of government from the colonial powers. Their weakness comprises lack of initiative, resourcefulness, organization and coordination in introducing authentically humanistic socio-political structures. They adopt party structures of the capitalist "mother country" without any modification. The proletariat which form part of the native political parties, as Fanon maintains, are characterized by "bourgeoise" mentality; they hold a privileged position among the colonized people. Furthermore, "the overwhelming majority of nationalist parties show a deep distrust toward the people of the rural areas"[2] which are static and feudal under the pacification of the colonial power. As Fanon comments:

> The political parties do not manage to organize the country districts. Instead of using existing structures and giving them a nationalist or progressive character, they mean to try and destroy living tradition in the colonial framework. They be-

lieve it lies in their power to give the initial impulse to the nation, whereas in reality the chains forged by the colonial system still weighs it down heavily.[3]

As one can see, Fanon considers rescuing "living tradition" as an integral part of decolonization. Colonial revolution is therefore a cultural revolution. Although the native "living tradition" is not ideal, it is a starting point for an authentic national culture which is progressive. The difficulty to be overcome is that the traditional societies are characterized, to a great extent, by disparity of "classes,"[4] whereas Fanon envisions a classless socialist socio-political structure. However, the colonial divide-and-rule policy must be eliminated.

Fanon further criticizes the nationalist parties for willing to break with colonialism and also wanting to be reconciled with it.[5] He thinks that authentic decolonization is irreconcilable with anything that colonialism stands for, because colonialism is essentially a negation of the humanity of the colonized. Consequently, the revolutionary minority in the party react by breaking away from the party legalism, which "shows itself opposed to any innovation."[6] They feel that "militating in a national party is not simply taking part in politics; it is choosing the only means whereby they can pass from the status of an animal to that of a human being."[7] Fanon also castigates the "bourgeoisie," the middle class in some developing nations for their single party system, "which is the modern form of the dictatorship of the bourgeoisie, unmasked, unpainted, unscrupulous, and cynical."[8] Their one party system is ridden with the corruption of instruments of power. It represents a change of the guards and not real revolution for the social welfare of all the people. In their self-seeking for personal aggrandisement, the national bourgeoisie establish the one party system which is "a national system of exploitation" in disguise. Lacking economic power, the bourgeoise leadership in the developing nation supplies the moral power for the members to get rich. It would be hard to contest Fanon's criticism. It has been said that the developing nations need a temporary dictatorship, "a stick" to bring the mass of the people in line with progress. Fanon is right in disagreeing. The influence of examples of selflessness and real love of the country is by no means a little motivating factor. However, there are some honest elements to help in redeeming the post independence situation. They are some intellectuals, "who have no precise ideas about politics, but who instinctively distrust the race of positions and which is symptomatic of the early days of independence in the colonized country."[9] These are to be deployed for the good of the nation.

2. DECENTRALIZATION AND SOCIALISM

To overcome the pitfall of the dictatorship of the bourgeoisie in the developing nations, Fanon proposes decentralization of authority in order to include the masses in the rural areas. A necessary step to decentralization is a nationalization of the middleman's trading sector which breeds the spirit of money-making and enjoyment of consumer goods. Fanon contends that the high taste for consumer goods on the part of the middle class creates a contempt for the masses. As Fanon writes:

> Nationalizing the intermediary sector means organizing wholesale and retail cooperatives on a democratic basis; it also means decentralizing these cooperatives by getting the mass of people interested in the ordering of public affairs. You will not be able to do all this unless you give the people some political education. . . . A government which declares that it wishes to educate the people politically thus expresses its desire to govern with the people for the people. It ought not to speak of language destined to camouflage a bourgeoise administration.[10]

One can see from this quotation that Fanon advocates a democratic socialist system as an ideal for the underdeveloped nations. He feels that this type of system is one that offers the opportunity for human development. His revolutionary humanism is primarily anchored in his concern for man, not as a tool for exploitation but as an end in himself. The redemption of the masses from exploitation and dehumanizing conditions of life is the redemption of humanity. Following Aristotle who maintains that man is a social being with a sense of justice flowing from his power of speech, Fanon argues that the masses have potentials for politics.

Although Fanon does not give a fully fledged description of the socialist ideal, it is fundamentally a policy oriented to the masses, the people. With a Rouseauist ring in his description, he maintains that the party should be an instrument for expressing the people's will:

> For the people, the party is not an authority, but an organism through which they as a people exercise their authority and express their will. The less there is of confusion and duality of powers, the more the party will play its part of guide and

the more securely it will constitute for the people a decisive guarantee.[11]

Fanon does not want the organization of political parties in the underdeveloped nations to follow the example of western systems because of their relegating the masses as incapable of self-government. According to him, a democratic socialist ideal maintains the pattern of social mobility and equal opportunity for men and women:

> Women will have exactly the same place as men, not in the clauses of the constitution but in the life of every day: in the factory, at school, and in the parliament.[12]

Attempts ought to be made to eradicate social evils such as hunger, poverty, ignorance, illiteracy, and to institute a program of educating the people from national consciousness to political and social consciousness. Programs for dealing with the distribution of wealth and with social relations are necessary.

With regard to the army, Fanon holds that the army should not be an autonomous body which may be engaged in politics and pose a threat to the government, but a servant of the nation. It should therefore not include professional soldiers, but be more of a militia. It is doubtful whether it will be very effective in modern warfare. However, the military rule that stalks the developing nations and distabilize them bear out Fanon's contention.

To sum up his socio-political ideal, it is better to do so in his words:

> . . . the choice of a socialist regime, a regime which is completely oriented toward the people as a whole and based on the principle that man is the most precious of all possessions, will allow us to go forward more quickly and more harmoniously, and thus make impossible that caricature of society where all economic and political power is held in the hands of a few who regard the nation as a whole with scorn and contempt.

He continues:

> We ought not to cultivate the exceptional or to seek for a hero who is another form of leader. We ought to uplift the people; we must develop their brains, fill them with ideas, change them and make them into human beings. . . . The masses should know that the government and the party are at their service. . .

> A government which calls itself a national government ought to take responsibility for the totality of the nation . . . The

national government, if it wants to be national, ought to govern by the people and for the people, for the outcasts and by the outcasts. No leader, however valuable he may be, can substitute himself for the popular will; and the national government, before concerning itself about international prestige, ought first to give back their dignity to the citizens, fill their minds and feast their eyes with human things, and create a prospect that is human because conscious and sovereign men dwell therein.[14]

This ideal gives meaning to his conception of revolution. He emphasizes government by participation rather than by representation. Although he virulently criticizes one party system as it was being developed in the newly independent nations, his ideal is still a decentralized one party system in which the grassroots participate through a kind of devolution of power (after political education) even in the remotest rural districts. At the grassroots level, an atmosphere should be generated for discussing the real needs of the people and how best to meet them. Thus, a "fruitful give-and-take from the bottom to the top and from the top to the bottom . . . creates and guarantees democracy in a party."[15] Concentration of power and resources in the capital should be decentralized to give life and movement to the rural districts, thereby arresting mass movement from the countryside to the capital. Rather than exploit the rural districts for the capital, the party should develop them with their raw material resources by building factories there. This will in no small measure restore the sense of human dignity to the masses.

Chapter IX
CONCLUDING REMARKS

Our discussion of Fanon's revolutionary humanism has revealed its many facets. The first part of our study is dominated by the resolution of the problem of reconciling violence with his humanism. Here violence is justified but not without great tension with the dialectical framework of self-defense on the part of the oppressed or colonized.

Contrary to the opinion of those who portray Fanon as a rabid revolutionary engaged in violence, he is a great humanist who is anguished in the dilemma of resolving the contradictions inherent in an oppresssive and dehumanizing system, specifically, the colonial system. He opted for violence as the last resort in order to achieve justice and humanity. His idea of humanizing or therapeutic function of violence appears paradoxical. As Aime Cesaire put it, "his violence . . . was that of the non-violent."[1] In the spectrum of violence, Fanon's attitude to violence is far from being an extreme one. He would agree that non-violence still remains the best means for resolving human problems. But non-violence appeared to be unavailing in the colonial world as he saw it. Today one can see that Fanon may be right in view of the fact that it is through the pressure of violence that the Rhodesian White minority under Mr. Ian Smith have come to a compromise to recognize the humanity of the Black majority in a universal suffrage. It may also be that only through the pressure of violence that the South African apartheid system will be transcended. It is regrettable that the latter has not become amenable to non-violent approaches.

Fanon's name reverberates among Black and White militants in the United States of America, and among prospective revolutionaries in the Developing Nations. As Peter Geisman commented, "his thoughts of the 1950's are central to black politics of the 1960's."[2] For example, he described Malcolm X's book, *Soul on Ice* "as Fanon coming home to roost."[3] Eldridge Cleaver's advice to Stokely Carmichael that "An undying love for black people that denies the humanity of other people is doomed."[4] is reminiscent of Fanon's criticism of Black racism. The danger in espousing Fanon's ideas is that many pick and choose in him, and lift him out of the context of his complex character. It is urgent to ask among his admirers whether he would agree that freedom must always be achieved by violent revolution. Is fight for freedom in the colonial system where the occupying power uses force and violence not different from the situation of an already independent nation? I think that there is a difference. One can work for change within a system without violent revolution.[5] The possibility of a threat of revolution can act as a lever for change for the better. The counsel of Fanon that we should change our ways for the better and be inventive in discovering ways of collaborating in building up the human world is in place. The program of liberating the oppressed is a case in point. There are, however, different ways of doing it according to the social and political circumstances, and in the light of progress already made.

Many of us are frightened on hearing of revolution and violence. I remember when I mentioned to a family friend of mine that I was making a critique of Fanon's conception of revolution, his wife was shocked: "Why write on revolution?" she asked. Fears are justified if they are not stifling and merely negative, but help us to do something. Revolutions shock us, if we are sincere, into doing something to prevent their causes: to attempt to erect just socio-political structures for the good of the human family. In this respect, it is not trivial to remark that action is mightier than words: "Do not curse the darkness but light a candle." This is the point which Fanon is making.

Fanon's project of "a new humanism" challenges the humanity of Black and White people. All men of good will, all with a sense of humanity should rally to save man from the cynicism of our time. Our human progress will ultimately resolve into mutual understanding, cooperation, communication and help to one another, and peace. The alternative to failure in erecting viable and good socio-political structures is endemic revolution and violence.

As to the question of Fanon rejecting Europe, one should view his rejection in the light of his project of authentically universalist humanism. With mixed feelings as I can read from the whole context of the last pages of *The Wretched of the Earth,* he criticizes European humanism for being vitiated by superiority complex, colonial imperialism, and wars and racism; it has become too particularized a phase in the dialectics of human history to represent the universality of the human kind, and consequently need be transcended by a humanism that really includes the humanity of the peoples in the Developing Nations. In the same vein, he condemns any socio-political system which does not recognize the human dignity of the grass-roots whether in Europe or in the Developing Nations. Specifically, he was appalled by the discrimination of Moslem Algerians against others, and by the internal power struggles which have resulted in dictatorial and military regimes in Africa. It has become a situation of Blacks over Blacks, but supported by some neo-colonialist powers.

It should be stressed that there is an undercurrent of reconciliation in Fanon's revolutionary humanism.[6] This undercurrent of reconciliation which springs from his analysis of Black and White relationship surfaces with full force in the closing paragraph of his last book, *The Wretched of the Earth.* He writes:

> For Europe, for ourselves, and for humanity, comrades, we must turn over a new leaf, we must work out new concepts, and try to set afoot a new man.[7]

As I have mentioned before, Socrates has said that "unexamined life is not worth living." His appeal for self-examination is a global one. Can we really be human if we inferiorize others. Fanon calls on Blacks and Whites to examine their conscience, and give up the ugliness of racial hatred and prejudice. With the spirit of reconciliation, we can envisage the withering away of revolutionary violence; thus non-violence becomes real.

In his preface to *The Wretched of the Earth,* Jean Paul Sartre asks Europe to listen to Fanon. He should be read with an open mind. He is indeed "a sign of contradiction" that is more apparent than real. Many have made a hero of him; many have repudiated him, and have preferred to catalogue his failures. Many are afraid to read him because of prejudice against revolution and revolutionaries. Yet his revolutionary humanism constitutes a critical source of the solution of some of our human problems today. Although he has not spoken the last word, he needs to be heard. As Roger Garaudy has significantly pointed up, "What we have to do is to work out an authentically universal humanism."[8] Fanon has attempted to map out a path in this direction in his revolutionary humanism. By critically investigating it, I have unraveled some of its problems and solutions. It is a stage toward an authentically universal humanism where violence will be replaced by non-violence; for, as we have seen, Fanon did not want to be a perpetual revolutionary.

It is important to note here that the authentic humanism that will form the atmosphere for the growth of Africa must take into account the spiritual and religious transcendence in African cultures: atheistic humanism falls short of the real expectations of Africa. And communism[9] which has been proposed by some thinkers is not the real answer to the problems of Africa and the rest of the Developing Nations. Christianity, with its thrust of universal love *(caritas)*, spiritual and religious transcendence, is not alien to African cultures; and since it has taken root in Africa, it has an essential role to play in the solution of African problems which are not only material. Secular humanism is not adequate for expressing the totality of African cosmology which includes an orientation to the divine, to God. The urgent task for African leaders and intellectuals is to find viable socio-political structures that will evolve from African traditions and uphold African values. Imitation of European systems is not enough for Africa to grow and contribute toward the good of humanity. It is appropriate to conclude with his soul-searching question:

Was my freedom not given to me then to build the world of you?[10]

BIOGRAPHICAL NOTES

1. Simone de Beauvoir: *La Force de Choses,* Vol. 2, Paris, Gallimard, 1963, p. 429. Quoted from Irene L. Gendzier, *Frantz Fanon,* p. 18.
2. See Irene Gendzier: *Frantz Fanon: A Critical Study,* pp. 10-11.
3. See Peter Geismar: *Fanon: A Biography,* p. 9.
4. *Ibid.,* p. 11.
5. See *Ibid.,* p. 65.
6. See a reprint of the speech, Frantz Fanon: *Toward the African Revolution,* pp. 31-44.
7. From a letter written in November to a friend in North Africa. The complete text of this letter is now in a new collection of Fanon's works, edited by C. Pirelli and published by Einaudi, Torino, Fall, 1970. My quotation is taken from Peter Geismar, *Fanon: A Biography,* p. 185.

SELECTED BIBLIOGRAPHY

Primary Sources

Fanon, Frantz: *Black Skin, White Masks.* Translated by Charles Lam Markmann, New York: Grove Press, Inc., 1967.

_____: *A Dying Colonization.* Translated from the French by Haakon Chevalier. New York: Grove Press, Inc., 1965.

_____: *Toward the African Revolution.* Translated by Haakon Chevalier. New York: Grove Press, Inc., 1967.

_____: *The Wretched of the Earth.* Translated by Constance Farrington. New York: Grove Press, Inc., 1965.

Zahar, Renate: *L'Oeuvre de Frantz Fanon.* Translated by R. Dangeville. Paris: Francois Maspero, 1970.

Secondary Sources

Bouvier, Pierre: *Fanon.* Paris: Editones Universitaires, 1971.

Caute, David: *Frantz Fanon.* New York: The Viking Press, 1970.

Cesaire, Aime: "The Homage to Frantz Fanon." *Presence Africaine,* Vol. 12, No. 40, 1962.

Domenache, Jean-Marie: "Les Damnes de la terre." *Espirit,* XXX, No. 305 (April, 1962), 634-645.

Forsythe, Dennis: "Frantz Fanon: Black Theoretician." *The Black Scholar,* I, No. 5 (March, 1970), 2-10.

Geismar, Peter and Peter Worsley: "Frantz Fanon: Evolution of a Revolutionary." *Monthly Review,* XXI, No. 1 (May, 1969), 22-49.

_____: *Fanon. A Biography.* New York: The Dial Press, 1971.

Gendzier, Irene L.: "Frantz Fanon: In Search of Justice." *Middle East Journal,* XX, No. 4 (Autumn, 1966), 534-544.

_____: *Frantz Fanon: A Critical Study.* New York: Pantheon Books, 1973.

Grohs, G.K.: "Frantz Fanon and the African Revolution." *The Journal of Modern African Studies,* VI, No. 4.

Guellal, Cherif: "Frantz Fanon: Prophet of Revolution." *Washington Post.* August 2, 1971, pp. B1 and B6.

Hansen, Emmanuel: *Frantz Fanon: Social and Political Thought.* Columbus, Ohio: Ohio State University Press, 1977.

Lucas, Philippe: *Sociologie de Frantz Fanon.* Algiers: SNED (Societe nationale d'edition et de diffusion), 1971.

Nghe, Nguyen: "Frantz Fanon et les problemes de l'independence." *La Pensee,* No. 107 (February, 1963), 23-36.

Onwuanibe, Richard: "Frantz Fanon: A Sign of Reconciliation or Contradiction." *Philosophical Form.* Vol. IX, Nos. 2-3, Fall/Winter, 1978/1979.

Siegel, J.E.: "On Frantz Fanon." *The American Scholar,* XXXVIII, No. 1 (Winter, 1968-69), 84-96.

Staniland, M.: "Frantz Fanon and the African Political Class." *African Affairs,* LXVIII, No. 270 (January, 1969).

Sutton, Horace: "Fanon: The Revolutionary as Prophet." *Saturday Review,* July 17, 1971, pp. 16-19, 59-60, New York: Saturday Review, Inc., 1971.

Zolberg, Aristede R.: "Frantz Fanon: A Gospel for the Damned." Encounter, XXVIII, No. 5 (November, 1966), 56-63.

_____: Aristede and Vera. "The Americanization of Frantz Fanon." The Public Interest, No. 9 (Fall, 1967), 49-63.

Philosophical Works

Books

Aquinas, St. Thomas: *Summa Theologiae.* Pt. 11-11, Q. 64, Art. 3. Translated by Fathers of the English Dominican Province, Vol. Two. New York/Boston/Cincinnati/Chicago/San Francisco, 1947.

Aristotle: *The Basic Works of Aristotle.* Edited by Richard McKeon. New York: Random House, 1961.

_____: *Nicomachaen Ethics.* New York: The Bobbs-Merrill Company, Inc., 1962.

Artz, Frederick Binkerd: *Renaissance Humanism.* Kent, Ohio: Kent State University Press, 1966.

Ayer, Alfred Jules (ed.): *The Humanist Outlook.* London Pemberton: Barrie and Rockliff, 1968.

Barker, Ernest, Sir (ed.): *Social Contract.* Oxford University Paperbacks. London, Oxford and New York: Oxford University Press, 1968.

Brandt, Richard B. (ed.): *Social Justice.* Englewood Cliffs, New Jersey: Prentice-Hall, Inc., 1962.

Calvert, Peter: *Revolution.* New York: Praeger Publishers, Inc., 1970.

Cassirer, Ernst: *An Essay on Man.* New Haven: Yale University Press, 1967.

Corliss, Lamont: *Humanism as a Philosophy.* New York: Philosophical Library, 1949.

de Beauvoir, Simone: *La Forces des Choses.* Paris: Gallimard, 1963. Translated from French by Richard Howard. *Force of Circumstances.* New York: Putnam, 1965.

De George, Richard T. (ed.): *Ethics and Society.* Anchor Books. New York: Doubleday and Company Inc., 1966.

Donagan, Alan H.: *The Theory of Morality.* Chicago: The University of Chicago Press, 1977.

Dresden, Sem: *Humanism in the Renaissance.* Translated from the Dutch by Margaret King. New York: McGraw Hill Book Company, 1968.

Ferguson, John: *Moral Values in the Ancient World.* New York: Barnes and Noble, Inc., 1959.

Feurer, Lewis S. (ed.): *Marx and Engles: Basic Writings on Politics and Philosophy.* Anchor Books. New York: Doubleday and Company, Inc.

Feuerback, Ludwig: *The Essence of Christianity.* Translated by George Eliot, New York: Harper Torchbooks, 1957.

Freire, Paulo: *Pedagogy of the Oppressed.* Translated by Myra Bergman Ramos. New York: The Seabury Press, 1973.

Friedrich, Carl J. (ed.): *Revolution.* (Nomos VIII). New York: Atherton Press, 1966.

————: (ed.): *The Philosophy of Hegel.* New York: The Modern Library.

Fromm, Erich (ed.): *Karl Marx: Selected Writings in Sociology and Social Philosophy.* Translated by T.B. Bottomore. McGraw Hill Paperbacks. New York: McGraw-Hill Book Company, Inc., 1964.

Garaudy, Roger: *Marxism in the Twentieth Century.* Translated by Rene Hague. New York: Charles Scribner's Sons, 1970.

Gray, Glenn J.: *On Understanding Violence Philosophically and Other Essays.* Harper Torchbooks. New York: Harper and Row, 1970.

Gross, Feliks: *The Seizure of Political Power in a Century of Revolutions.* New York: The Philosophical Library, 1958.

Guthrie, S.K.C., *The Sophists.* Cambridge: At the University Press, 1971.

Hadas, Moses: *Humanism: The Greek Ideal and Its Survival.* New York: Harper, 1960.

Hegel, G.W.F.: *The Phenomenology of Mind.* Translated by Sir James B. Baillie, Harper Torchbooks. New York: Harper and Row, 1967.

————: *Philosophy of Right.* Translated with notes by T.M. Knox, London, Oxford and New York: Oxford University Press, 1967.

————: *Reason in History.* Translated by Robert S. Hartman. New York: The Bobbs-Merrill Company, Inc., 1953.

Jaeger, Werner: *Paideia: The Ideals of Greek Culture.* Translated by Gilbert Highet, Vols. I and II. 1939-1943.

Jaszi, O., and J.D. Lewis: *Against the Tyrant.* Glencoe, Illinois: New Press, 1957.

Josephson, Eric and Mary (eds.): *Man Alone: Alienation in Modern Society.* A Laurel Paperback Edition. New York: Dell Publishing Company, Inc., 1962.

Kant, Immanuel: *Critique of Practical Reason.* A Liberal Arts Press Book (Paperback). Indianapolis and New York: The Bobbs-Merrill Company Inc., 1956.

Lasswell, Harold D., and Daniel Lerner (eds.): *World Revolutionary Elites: Studies in Coercive Ideological Movements.* Cambridge: The M.I.T. Press, 1965.

Levi, Albert William: *Humanism and Politics.* Bloomington, Indiana: University Press, 1969.

Machiavelli, Niccolo: *The Prince.* Translated and Edited by Thomas G. Bergin. New York: F.S. Crofts and Company, Inc., 1947.

Macky, Peter W.: *Violence: Right or Wrong?* Waco, Texas: Word Books, Publishers, Inc., 1973.

Marck, Van der: *Love and Fertility: Contemporary Questions About Birth Regulation.* London/New York, 1965.

Maritain, Jacques: *True Humanism.* Translated by M.R. Adamson. London: Geoffrey Bles: The Centenary Press, 1936.

————: *Man and the State.* Chicago: The University of Chicago Press, 1971.

Marx, Karl and Frederick Engels: *Early Writings*. Translated and Edited by T.B. Bottomore. McGraw-Hill Paperbacks. New York, Toronto, and London: McGraw-Hill Book Company, 1964.

_____: *Selected Writings in Sociology and Social Science*. Translated by T.B. Bottomore. Edited by Bottomore and Maximilien Rubel. McGraw-Hill Book Company, 1964.

_____: *The German Ideology*. New World Paperbacks. New York: International Publishers, 1969.

Merleau-Ponty, Maurice: *Phenomenology of Perception*. Translated from the French by Colin Smith. New York: The Humanities Press, 1967.

_____: *Humanism and Terror*. Boston: Beacon Press, 1969.

Mezu, Okechukwu S.: *The Philosophy of Pan-Africanism*. Washington D.C., Georgetown University Press, 1965.

Nelson, Truman: *Right of Revolution*. Boston: Beacon Press, Inc., 1968.

Nisbet, Robert A.: *The Social Philosophers: Community and Conflict in Western Thought*. New York: Crowell, 1975.

Novack, George (ed.): *Their Morals and Ours. Marxist Versus Liberal Views on Morality*. New York: Merit Publishers, Inc., 1969.

Plato: *The Collected Dialogues*. Edited by Edith Hamilton and Huntington Cairne. New York: Bollington Foundation, 1961.

Raphael, D.D.: *Problems of Political Philosophy*. New York: Praeger Publishers, Inc., 1971.

Rees, John: *Equality*. New York, Washington and London: Praeger Publishers, Inc., 1971.

Sartre, Jean-Paul: *Critique de la raison dialectique, precede de Question methode*. Paris: Gallimard, 1960.

_____: *Orphee Noir: Preface a l'anthologie de la nouvelle poesie engre et malgache*. Paris: Presses Universitaires de France, 1948.

Schacht, Richard: *Alienation*, Garden City, New York: Doubleday and Company, Inc., 1971.

Shaffer, Jerome A. (ed.): *Violence*. New York: David McKay Company, Inc., 1971.

Sommerville, John: *Violence*. New York: David McKay Company, Inc., 1971.

Sorel, Georges: *Reflections on Violence*. Translated by T.E. Hulme and J. Roth. Collier Books. New York: The Macmillan Company, 1967.

Wasserstrom, Richard (ed.): *War and Morality*. Belmont, California: Wadsworth Publishing Company, Inc., 1970.

West, Charles C.: *Ethics, Violence and Revolution*. Special Studies No. 208. New York: The Council on Religion and International Affairs, 1969.

Zeller, Eduard: *Outlines of the History of Greek Philosophy*. New York: The World Publishing Company, Inc., 1955.

Articles

Anscombe, Elizabeth: "War and Murder." *War and Morality*. Edited by Richard A. Wasserstrom. Belmont, California: Wadsworth Publishing Company, Inc., 1970.

Azikiwe, Ben N.: "Ethics of Colonial Imperialism." *Journal of Negro History*, XVI, No. 3 (July, 1931), 287-309.

Dupre, Louis K.: "The Concept of Alienation in Hegel Compared to Its Reinterpretation in Marx." Unpublished Paper Presented at Class Lecture. Washington D.C.: Georgetown University, 1969.

Ford, John C., S.J.: "The Morality of Obliteration Bombing." *War and Morality.* Edited by Richard A. Wasserstrom. Belmont, California: Wadsworth Publishing Company, Inc., 1970.

Ghoos, J.: "L'Acte a Double Effect: Etude de Theologie Positive." *Ephemerides Theologiae Lovaniensis,* XXVII (1951).

Grisez, Germain G.: "Toward a Consistent Natural Law Ethics of Killing." *The American Journal of Jurisprudence,* Vol. 15 (1970).

Knauer, Peter, S.J.: "The Hermeneutics Function of the Principle of Double Effect." *Natural Law Forum,* 12 (1967).

Lasky, Melvin J.: "The Birth of a Metaphor: On the Origins of Utopia and Revolution." 2 Pts. Pt. I, Encounter, XXXIV, No. 2 (February, 1970), 35-45. Pt. II, Encounter, XXXIV, No. 3 (March, 1970), 30-42.

Mangan, Joseph T., S.J.: "An Historical Analysis of the Principle of Double Effect." *Theological Studies,* X (1949).

Moore, Barrington, Jr.: "On the Notions of Progress, Revolution, and Freedom." *Ethics,* LXXII, No. 2 (January, 1962), 106-119.

Naeveson, Jan: "Pacifism: A Philosophical Analysis." *War and Morality.* Edited by Richard Wasserstrom. Belmont, California: Wadsworth Publishing Company, Inc., 1970.

Wolff, Robert P.: "On Violence." *Journal of Philosophy,* 66, No. 19 (2 October 1969).

General Works

Books

Arendt, Hannah: *Imperialism Part II.* A Harvest Book. New York: Harcourt, Brace and World, Inc., 1951.

———————: *On Violence.* New York: Harcourt, Brace and World, Inc., 1969.

Ibid., On Revolution. New York: The Viking Press, 1965.

Aron, Robert, *et al.: Les Origines de la guerre d'Algerie.* Paris: Fayard, 1962.

Bienen, Henry: *Violence and Social Change: A Review of Current Literature.* Chicago: The University of Chicago Press, 1968.

Bocca, Geoffrey: *The Secret Army.* Englewood Cliffs, New Jersey: Prentice-Hall-Inc., 1968.

Brogan, Dennis W.: *The Price of Revolution.* New York: Harper and Row Publishers, Inc., 1951.

Burns, Sir Alan: *Colour Prejudice.* London: G. Allen and Unwin, Ltd., 1948.

Cartey, Wilfred and Martin Kilson (eds.): *The Africa Reader: Colonial Africa.* New York: Vintage Books, 1970.

Cary, Joyce: *The Case for African Freedom.* Austin: University of Texas Press, 1962.

Cesaire, Aime: *Return to My Native Land.* Translated by John Berger and Anna Bostock. (Cahier d'm retour au pays natal.) Baltimore: Penguin Books, Inc., 1969.

Chalmers, Johnson: *Revolution and the Social System.* Hoover Institution Studies No. 3. Stanford, California: Stanford University Press, 1964.

_____: *Revolutionary Change*. Boston: Little, Brown and Company, 1967.

Clark, Leon E.: *Through African Eyes: Cultures in Change Unit IV. Colonial Experience*. New York: Frederick A. Praeger, Publishers, 1970.

Clark, Michael K.: *Algeria in Turmoil: A History of the Rebellion*. New York: Frederick A. Praeger, Publishers, 1959.

Cleaver, Eldridge: *Soul on Ice*. New York: Dell, 1968.

Corbett, Edward M.: *The French Presence in Black Africa*. Washington, Black Orpheus Press, 1972.

Coser, A. Lewis: *Continuities in the Study of Social Conflict*. New York: Free Press, 1967.

Cranston, Maurice: *What are Human Rights?* New York: Basic Books, Inc., Publishers, 1962.

Dunn, John: *Modern Revolutions*. Cambridge: Cambridge University Press, 1972.

Eckstein, Harry (ed.): *Internal War, Problems and Approaches*. New York: The Free Press, 1964.

Eichelberger, William L.: *Reality in Black and White*. Philadelphia: The Westminster Press.

Ellul, Jacques: *Violence*. Translated by Cecelia Gaul Kings. New York: Seabury Press, 1969.

Freud, Anna: *The Ego and the Mechanism of Defense*. New York: International University Press, 1946.

Gerassi, John (ed.): *Towards Revolution*. Vols. 1 and 2. London: Weidenfeld and Nicolson, 1971.

Gillespie, Joan: *Algeria: Rebellion and Revolution*. New York: Frederick A. Praeger, Inc., 1961.

Gilmore, Myron Piper: *The World of Humanism. 1453-1517*. New York: Harper, 1952.

Ginewski, Paul: *The Two Faces of Apartheid*. Chicago: Henry Regency Company, 1965.

Gordon, David C.: *North Africa's French Legacy, 1954-1962*. Harvard Middle Eastern Monograph. Cambridge: Distributed for the Center for Middle Eastern Studies of Harvard University by Harvard University Press, 1962.

_____: *The Passing of French Algeria*. London: Oxford University Press, 1966.

Grier, William H., and Price M. Cobbs: *Black Rage*. New York: Basic Books, 1968.

Hallet, Robin: *The Penetration of Africa*. New York: Frederick A. Praeger Publishers, Inc., 1967.

Heggoy, Alf Andrew: *Insurgency and Counterinsurgency in Algeria*. Bloomington/London: Indiana University Press, 1972.

Henissart, Paul: *Wolves in the City: The Death of French Algeria*. New York: Simon and Schuster, 1970.

Hobson, John Atkinson: *Imperialism, A Study*. London: G. Allen and Unwin, Ltd., 1948.

Hodges, Donald Clark: *Socialist Humanism*. St. Louis, Missouri: Warren H. Green, Inc., 1974.

Jalee, Pierre: *The Pillage of the Third World*. Translated from the French by

Mary Klopper. Modern Reader Paperback. New York: Monthly Review Press, 1970.

Jaspers, Karl: *The Future of Mankind.* Translated by E.B. Ashton. Phoenix Books. Chicago: University of Chicago Press, 1961.

Jordan, Winthrop, D.: *The White Man's Burden. Historical Origins of Racism in the United States.* London, Oxford, New York: Oxford University Press, 1974.

Jouvenel, Bertrand de: *On Power.* Boston: Beacon Press, 1962.

Kluckhohn, Clyde: *Mirror for Man.* A Premier Book. Chapter 5, "Race: A Modern Myth." Greenwich, Connecticut: Fawcett Publications, Inc., 1965.

Langer, William Leonard: *The Diplomacy of Imperialism.* New York: Alfred A. Knopf, 1951.

Leakey, L.S.B.: *Defeating Mau Mau.* London: Methuen and Company, Ltd., 1954.

Legjaoui, Mohamed: *Verites sur la Revolution algerienne.* Paris: Editions Gallimard, 1970.

Legune, Colin: *Pan-Africanism.* New York: Frederick A. Praeger, Inc., 1962.

Leiden, Carl and Karl M. Schmitt: *The Politics of Violence.* A Spectrum Book. Englewood Cliffs, New Jersey: Prentice-Hall, Inc., 1968.

Lester, Julius, ed.: *The Thought and Writings of W.E.B. DuBois.* New York: Vintage Books, 1971.

Lewis, William H. (ed.): *French Speaking Africa: The Search for Identity.* Walker Paperback. New York: Walker and Company, 1965.

Lintott, H.W.: *Violence in Republic Rome.* Oxford: Clarendon Press, 1968.

Lorenz, Konrad: *On Aggression.* Translated by Marjorie Kerr Wilson. New York: Bantam Books, Inc., 1967.

Mallin, Jay: *Terror and Urban Guerrillas.* Coral Gables: University of Miami Press, 1971.

Mannoni, Dominique O.: *Prospero and Calihan: The Psychology of Colonization.* New York: Frederick A. Praeger, Inc., 1961.

Mazlish, Bruce (ed.): *Revolution: A Reader.* New York: The Macmillan Company, 1971.

Mazzeo, Joseph Anthony: *Renaissance and Revolution.* New York: Pantheon Books, Inc., 1969.

Memmi, Albert: *The Colonizer and the Colonized.* A Beacon Paperback. Translated from the French by Howard Greenfeld. Boston: Beacon Press, 1969.

Montagu, Ashley: *Race, Science and Humanity.* An Insight Book. New York: Van Nostrand Reinhold Company, 1963.

Moon, Parker Thomas: *Imperialism and World Politics.* New York: The Macmillan Company, 1926.

Morris, Richard B.: *The Emerging Nations and the American Revolution.* New York: Harper and Row, Publishers, Inc., 1970.

O'Ballance, Edgar: *The Algerian Insurrection, 1954-1962.* Hamden, Connecticut: Anchor Books, 1967.

Ottaway, David and Marina: *Algeria: The Politics of a Socialist Revolution.* Berkeley and Los Angeles: The University of California Press, 1970.

Paret, Peter: *French Revolutionary Warfare from Indochina to Algeria.* New York: Frederick A. Praeger, Inc., 1968.

Paul VI, Pope: *On the Development of Peoples.* New York: Paulist Press, 1967.

Pettee, George Sawyer: *The Process of Revolution.* New York: Harper and Row, Publishers, 1938.

Pettigrew, Thomas F.: *A Profile of the Negro American.* New York: D. Van Nostrand Company, Inc., 1964.

Quandt, William B.: *Revolution and Political Leadership: Algeria, 1954-1968.* Cambridge, Massachusetts: The M.I.T. Press, 1969.

Quaison-Sackey, Alex: *Africa Unbound.* New York: Frederick A. Praeger, Inc., 1963.

Ralph, Philip Lee: *The Renaissance in Perspective.* New York: St. Martin's Press, Inc., 1973.

Robinson, Ronald and John Gallagher: *Africa and the Victorians.* Garden City, New York: Anchor Books (Doubleday and Company, Inc.), 1968.

Ross, James Bruce and Mary Martin McLaughlin (ed.): *The Portable Renaissance Reader.* New York: The Viking Press, Inc., 1972.

Ross, James Robert (ed.): *The War Within. Violence or Non-violence in the Black Revolution.* New York: Steed and Ward, Inc., 1971.

Said, Abdul A., and Daniel M. Collier: *Revolutionism.*

Sartre, Jean Paul: *Anti-Semite and Jew.* Translated by George J. Becker. New York: Schocker Books, 1948.

——————: *Black Orpheus.* Translated by S.W. Allen. Paris: Prescence Africaine, n.d.

——————: *The Reprieve.* Translated from the French by Eric Sutton. New York: A.A. Knopf, 1947.

Snyder, Louis L. (ed.): *The Idea of Racialism.* An Anvil Book. Princeton, New Jersey: D. Van Nostrand Company, Inc., 1962.

Storr, Anthony: *Human Aggression.* A Bantam Book. New York: Atheneum Publishers, 1968.

Tillion, Germaine: *France and Algeria.* Translated by R. Howard. New York: Alfred A. Knopf, 1961.

Tripier, Philippe: *Autopsie de la Guerre d'Algerie.* Paris: Editions France-Empire, 1972.

Wieschoff, H.A.: *Colonial Policies in Africa.* Philadelphia: University of Pennsylvania Press, 1944.

Winslow, E.M.: *The Pattern of Imperialism: A Study in Theories of Power.* New York: Columbia University, 1944.

Articles

Amann, Peter: "Revolution: A Redefinition." *Political Science Quarterly.* LXVII, No. 1 (March, 1962), 36-53.

Calvert, P.A.R.: "Revolution: The Politics of Violence." *Political Studies,* XV, No. 1 (February, 1967), 1-11.

Dvorin, Eugene P.: "Problems of Colonialism and Imperialism in Sub-Saharan Africa." *United Asia.* VII, No. 5 (October, 1955), 250-259.

Eckstein, Harry: "On the Etiology of Internal Wars," in *Revolution: A Reader.* Bruce Mazlish (ed.). New York: The Macmillan Company, 1971, pp. 18-44.

Fitch, Robert E.: "The Uses of Violence." *Christian Century.* 85 (7 April 1968).

Griewank, Karl: "Emergence of the Concept of Revolution," in *Revolution: A Reader*. Edited by Bruce Mazlish, New York: The Macmillan Company, 1971 pp. 1-18.

Hatto, Arthur: "Revolution: An Enquiry into the Usefulness of an Historical Term." *Mind,* New Series, 58 (October, 1949), p. 295.

Neumann, Sigmund: "The Internal Civil War," *World Politics,* Vol. 1 (1949).

Stone, Lawrence: "Theories of Revolution," in *Revolution: A Reader*. Edited by Bruce Mazlish. New York: The Macmillan Company, 1971, pp. 44-57.

Wright, Peter: "Development of Political Unrest in Africa," *United Asia,* VII, No. 2 (March, 1955), 102-106.

Yoder, Dale: "Current Definitions of Revolutions." *The American Journal of Sociology,* Vol. 32 (1926), 433-441.

Zeitlin, M.: "Alienation and Revolution." *Social Forces,* SLV, No. 2 (December, 1966), 224-236.

NOTES

Preface

1. Lewis A. Coser: *Continuities in the Study of Conflict* (New York: Free Press, 1967), p. 213.
2. Robert Nisbet: *The Social Philosophers: Community and Conflict in Western Thought* (New York: Crowell, 1975), p. 306.
3. J.E. Siegel: "On Frantz Fanon," *The American Scholar,* Winger 1968-69, p. 85.
4. Frantz Fanon: *Black Skin, White Masks,* trans. by Charles Lam Markmann (New York: Grove Press, Inc., 1967), p. 231.

Chapter I

1. See Leone Battista Alberti: "Self-Portrait of a Universal Man," *The Portable Renaissance Reader,* pp. 480 ff. for a description of this type.
2. See Werner Jaeger: *Paideia: The Ideals of Greek Culture,* translated by Gilbert Higbet, Vols. I—II (1939-1943); and Joseph Anthony Mazzeo, *Renaissance and Revolution* (New York: Pantheon Books, Inc., 1966), Chapter 1.
3. See for example, Erasmus: *The Education of a Christian Prince;* Thomas More, *Utopia;* and Salutati, *De Tyranno.*
4. Corliss Lamont: *Humanism as a Philosophy* (New York: Philosophy Library, 1949) p. 7.
5. See Giovanni Pico Della Mirandola: "The Dignity of Man" (1486), *Portable Renaissance Reader,* pp. 476-479.
6. Frantz Fanon: *Black Skin, White Masks,* p. 8.
7. *Ibid,* p. 222.
8. Revolution was originally used as an astronomical term for describing revolving movements of the heavenly bodies following inexorable laws. It has taken on social and political meaning as a metaphor from astronomy to denote the movement of revolving back to a pre-established order. See Melvin J. Laskey, "The Birth of Metaphor: On the Origin of Utopia and Revolution," 2 pts.: Pt. 1, *Encounter,* XXXIV, No. 2.
9. Peter Calvert: *Revolution* (New York: Praeger Publishers, Inc., 1970), p. 18.
10. See *Ibid.,* p. 26.
11. See Dennis Brogan who says that as "concept, as reality, revolution is one of the oldest institutions in our Western civilization." *The Price of Revolution* (New York: Harper and Row Publishers, 1951), p. 1.
12. Aristotle: *Politics,* 1301b 5-10.
13. *Ibid.,* 1304b5.
14. See Calvert: *Op. Cit.* p. 39.
15. H.W. Lintoth: *Violence in Republican Rome* (Oxford: Clarendon Press, 1968), p. 52. Quoted from Calvert, Op. Cit., p. 39.
16. See Arthur Hatto: "Revolution: An Enquiry into the Usefulness of an Historical Term," *Mind,* 58 (October, 1949), p. 295. Quoted from Calvert, Op. Cit., p. 39.
17. Charles A. Ellwood: *The Psychology of Human Society,* pp. 20-21.
18. Johnson Chalmers: *Revolution and Social System,* Hoover Institution Studies 3 (Stanford, Calif: Stanford University Press, 1964), p. 10.

19. Peter Calvert: "Revolution: The Politics of Violence," *Political Studies,* Vol. 15 (1927), p. 1.

20. Harry Eckstein: "On the Etiology of Internal Wars," *Revolution: A Reader,* ed. by Bruce Mazlish, p. 21.

21. Eugene Kameka: "The Concept of a Political Revolution," *Revolutions,* ed. by Carl Friedrich, p. 124.

22. See Fanon: *The Wretched of the Earth,* translated by Constance Farrington (New York: Grove Press, Inc., 1965), pp. 35 ff. for detail.

23. Hannah Arendt: *On Revolution* (New York: The Viking Press, 1965), p. 28.

24. Fanon: *The Wretched of the Earth,* p. 35.

25. Robert P. Wolff: "On Violence," *Journal of Philosophy* 66, No. 19 (2 October 1969) p. 606.

26. Ronald B. Miller: "Violence, Force and Coercion," *Violence,* ed. by Jerome A. Shaffer, p. 25.

27. Robert Audi: "On the Meaning and Justification of Violence," *Violence,* ed. by Jerome A. Shaffer, p. 59.

28. Robert E. Fitch: "The Uses of Violence," *Christian Century,* 85 (7 April 1968), p. 483.

29. Barbara Deming: "On Revolution and Equilibrium," *The War Within,* ed. by James Robert Ross, p. 154.

30. Fanon: *The Wretched of the Earth,* p. 37.

31. Italics are mine.

32. Fanon: *The Wretched of the Earth,* p. 147.

33. For a good discussion of the distinction between violence, force, coercion, and pressure see Ronald B. Miller, *Op Cit.* pp. 30—33; and Peter W. Macky, *Violence: Right or Wrong?,* pp. 22—23.

34. Fanon: *The Wretched of the Earth.* Georges Sorel and Jean-Paul Sartre are in this tradition: see Georges Sorel: *Reflections on Violence,* trans. by T.E. Hulme and J. Roth (New York: The Macmillan Company, 1967), pp. 180-215; Jean-Paul Sartre: *Critique of Dialectical Reason.*

35. Fanon: *The Wretched of the Earth,* p. 36.

36. *Ibid.,* p. 36.

37. Irene L. Gendzier: *Frantz Fanon: A Critical Study* (New York: Pantheon Books, 1973), p. 201.

Chapter II

1. See Jean-Paul Sartre: "Preface," *The Wretched of the Earth,* p. 7.

2. Plato: *Apology,* 38a.

3. *Politics,* 1254b 15—20.

4. DP 1364, fr. 2, DK fr. 44B. (Quoted from W.K.C. Guthrie, *The Sophists* (Cambridge: At the University Press, 1971), p. 153.

5. W.K.C. Guthrie: *The Sophists,* p. 156.

6. *Ibid.,* p. 159.

7. See Fanon: *Black Skin, White Masks,* p. 229.

8. G.W.F. Hegel: *The Phenomenology of Mind,* trans. by Sir James B. Baillie (New York: Harper and Row, 1967), p. 229.

9. Immanuel Kant: *Critique of Practical Reason* (Indianapolis and New York: Bobbs-Merrill Company, Inc., 1956), p. 90.

10. See Hegel, *Op. Cit.*, pp. 229—240.

11. *Ibid.*, p. 233.

12. *Ibid.*, p. 231.

13. See Fanon: *Black Skin, White Masks*, p. 217.

14. *Ibid.*, p. 217.

15. *Ibid.*, p. 218.

16. *Ibid.*, p. 218.

17. *Ibid.*, p. 219.

18. *Ibid.*, p. 221. This is a Kierkegaardian concept.

19. See Fanon: *Toward the African Revolution,* trans. by Haakon Chevalier (New York: Grove Press, Inc., 1967), p. 114.

20. See Anthony Storr: *Human Aggression* (New York: Antheneum Publishers, 1968), p. 42 ff. See also Konrad Lorenz, *On Aggression,* trans. by Marjorie Kerr Wilson (New York: Bantam Books, Inc., 1967), pp. 20 ff. for an account of the positive function of aggression in animals. But care must be taken not to extrapolate too much from the environment of animals.

21. See Hegel: *Philosophy of History*, p. 18.

22. Fanon: *Black Skin, White Masks*, p. 30.

23. *Ibid.*, pp. 230—231.

24. *Ibid.*, p. 230.

25. *Ibid.*, p. 230.

26. *Ibid.*, p. 231.

27. *Ibid.*, pp. 231—232.

28. See Socrates' argument with Thrasymachus, Plato: *Republic*, I, 337a ff.

29. See Aristotle: *Ethics*, 1131a 10 ff.

30. Plato: *Laws*, 757a.

31. Gregory Vlastos: "Justice and Equality," *Social Justice*, ed. by Richard Brandt, p. 40.

32. William K. Frankena: "'The Concept of Social Justice," *Social Justice*, ed. by Richard B. Brandt, p. 13.

33. Ernest Barker, ed.: *Social Contract* (London and New York: Oxford University Press, 1968), footnote, p. 189.

34. *Ibid.*, p. 173.

35. *Ibid.*, p. 177.

36. Fanon, *Toward the African Revolution*, pp. 83 ff.

37. *Ibid.*, p. 53.

38. *Ibid.*, p. 54.

39. Aristotle: *Nicomachean Ethics*, 1155a20-25; see Robert O. Johann, "Love and Justice," *Ethics and Society*, ed. by R.T. DeGeorge, pp. 25 ff; John Ferguson, *Moral Values in the Ancient World*, Chapter VII.

40. Fanon: *Black Skin, White Masks*, p. 231.

41. *Ibid.*, p. 8.

42. *Ibid.*, p. 8.

43. *Ibid.*, p. 9.

44. *Ibid.*, p. 226.
45. Fanon, *Toward the African Revolution,* p. 114.
46. *Ibid.*, p. 144.
47. *Ibid.*, p. 126.
48. See George Novak, ed.: *Their Morals and Ours. Marxist Versus Liberal Views* on Morality (New York: Merit Publishers, Inc., 1969).
49. *Op. Cit.,* p. 316; italics are mine.
50. See St. Paul: 2 Cor. 5:17; Col. 3:10-11; Eph. 4:23-24.
51. Carl J. Freidrich (ed.): *The Philosophy of Hegel.* New York: The Modern Library, p. 194.
52. See G.W.F. Hegel: *Reason in History,* trans. by Robert S. Hartman (New York: The Bobbs-Merrill Company, Inc., 1953), pp.22-25.
53. Fanon: *Toward the African Revolution,* p. 170.
54. Fanon: *Black Skin, White Masks,* p. 113.
55. Fanon: *Toward the African Revolution,* p. 170.
56. *Ibid.*, p. 173.
57. *Ibid.*, pp. 33 ff.
58. *Ibid.*, p. 33.
59. *Ibid.*, p. 38.
60. *Ibid.*, p. 41.
61. *Ibid.*, p. 43.
62. *Ibid.*, p. 44.

Chapter III

1. Fanon conducted sociotherapeutic experiments on the inmates of the psychiatric hospital in Blida, Algeria.
2. See Fanon: *Toward the African Revolution,* p. 54.
3. Eric and Mary Josephson, eds.: *Man Alone; Alienation in Modern Society* (New York: Dell Publishing Company, Inc., 1962), p. 12.
4. See Richard Schacht: *Alienation* (New York: Doubleday and Company, Inc., 1971), p. 43 ff.
5. G.W.F. Hegel: *The Phenomenology of Mind,* p. 457.
6. *Ibid.*, p. 513.
7. *Ibid.*, p. 525.
8. *Ibid.*, p. 526.
9. "Die Verfassung Deutschlands." (13) Quoted from Schacht, *op. cit.,* p. 34.
10. Schacht: *op. cit.,* pp. 35-36.
11. This is debatable because true religion stipulates love of one's neighbour works of charity and justice.
12. See Feuerbach: *The Essence of Christianity,* trans. by George Eliot (New York: Harper Torchbooks, 1957).
13. T.B. Bottomore, ed.: *Karl Marx: Early Writings* (New York: McGraw-Hill Book Company, 1964) p. 198.
14. Fanon: *Black Skin, White Masks,* p. 202.
15. Fanon: *The Wretched of the Earth,* p. 40.

16. Fanon: *Black Skin, White Masks,* p. 44.

17. See Louis L. Snyder: *The Idea of Racialism* (Princeton, New Jersey: D. Van Nostrand Company, Inc., 1962), for a collection of these myths. An attempt is made to show the wrong-headedness of these myths.

18. See Ashley Montagu, *Race, Science and Humanity* (New York: Van Nostrand Reinhold Company, 1963), especially "Scientific Racism," pp. 136-145, which shows up the false basis of the so-called "scientific facts" as the justification for racism. See also Thomas F. Pettigrew, *A Profile of the Negro American.* Princeton, New Jersey: D. Van Nostrand Company, Inc., 1964), Chs. 3 and 5 for the refutation of the alleged mental inferiority of the American Negro. He quotes the following resolution of the American Anthropological Association in 1961 (p. 131):

> The American Anthropological Association repudiates state-
> ments now appearing in the United States that Negroes are
> biologically and in innate mental ability inferior to whites, and
> reaffirms the fact that there is no scientifically established evi-
> dence to justify the exclusion of any race from rights guaran-
> teed by the Constitution of the United States. The basic prin-
> ciple of equality of opportunity and equality before the law are
> compatible with all that is known about human biology. All races
> possess the ability needed to participate fully in the democratic
> way of life and in modern technological civilization.

Cf. Also Clyde Kluckhohn, *Mirror for Man* (Greenwich, Connecticut: Faw-cett Publications, Inc., 1965), Ch. 5, "Race: A Modern Myth."

19. See Fanon: *Black Skin, White Masks,* pp. 93 ff.

20. See *Ibid.,* p. 170.

21. See *Ibid.,* pp. 17 ff.

22. See *Ibid.,* pp. 17-18.

23. See *Ibid.,* pp. 41 ff.

24. See *Ibid.,* pp. 41 ff.

25. See *Ibid.,* p. 63.

26. Quoted from Fanon: *Black Skin, White Masks,* p. 42.

27. *Ibid.,* p. 41.

28. *Ibid.,* p. 44.

29. *Ibid.,* p. 191.

30. See Jean-Paul Sartre: *Anti-Semite and Jew,* trans. by George J. Becker (New York: Schocken Books, 1948).

31. See Jean-Paul Sartre: *The Reprieve,* trans. by Eric Sutton (New York: A.A. Knopf, 1947).

32. Fanon: *Black Skin, White Masks,* p. 194.

33. Its positive recognition of its skin has taken on the form of negritude.

34. Fanon: *The Wretched of the Earth,* p. 41.

35. *Ibid.,* pp. 55 ff.

36. Fanon: *Black Skin, White Masks,* pp. 223-224.

37. See Wilfred Cartey and Martin Kilson, eds.: *The Africa Reader: Colonial Africa* (New York: Vintage Books, 1970); Leon E. Clark, ed.: *Through African Eyes: Cultures in Change,* Unit IV, *Colonial Experience* (New York: Freder-ick A. Praeger, Publishers, 1970); Ronald Robinson and John Gallagher:

Africa and the Victorians: The Climax of Imperialism (Garden City, New York: Doubleday and Company, Inc., 1968).

38. See Ben N. Azikiwe: "Ethics of Colonial Imperialism," *Journal of Negro History,* pp. 298-309; Albert Memmi: *The Colonizer and the Colonized,* trans. by Howard Greenfeld (Boston: Beacon Press, 1969), which is a reflection on the theme which Fanon reflects on. In this connection see also Karl Jaspers: *End of Colonialism, The Future of Mankind,* pp. 67-71; Wilfred Cartey and Martin Kilson, *op. cit.,* for an account of the native reaction to the conquest and adaptation to the colonial rule; Eugene P. Dvorin, "Problems of Colonialism and Imperialism in Sub-Saharan Africa," *United Asia,* VII, No. 5, pp. 250-259; Robin Hallet: *The Penetration of Africa* (New York: Frederick A. Praeger Publishers, Inc., 1967); Sir Harry H. Johnson: *A History of the Colonization of Africa.* See also Hannah Arendt: *Imperialism,* Part II (New York: Harcourt, Brace and World, Inc., 1951).

39. E.M. Winslow: *The Pattern of Imperialism: A Study of the Theories of Power* (New York: Columbia University Press, 1944), p. 15.

40. Malachy Postlethwayt: *Britain's Commercial Interest Explained and Improved* (London: Browne), p. 153. Quoted from Winslow, Op. Cit., p. 141.

41. E.M. Winslow, *Op. Cit.,* p. 67. See Hannah Arendt, *op. cit.,* pp. 38-101; Louis Snyder: *The Imperialism Reader* (New York: D. Van Nostrand Company, Inc., 1962).

42. John A. Hobson: *Imperialism: A Study* (London: G. Allen and Unwin, Ltd., 1948). p. 232. See also Louis L. Snyder: "The Anglo-Saxon Myth: The White Man's Burden," *The Idea of Racialism,* pp. 54-61; Moritz Julius Bonn: "Race and Imperialism," *The Idea of Racialism,* pp. 123-125; Winthrop D. Jordan: *The White Man's Burden: Historical Origins of Racism in the United States* (London and New York: Oxford University Press, 1974).

43. See Karl Jaspers: *Op. Cit.,* pp. 67-71.

44. See Pierre Jalee: "The Pillage of the Third World," *Monthly Review Press* (New York, 1968).

45. This is the policy of all British and Dutch Colonialists. In North America the Indians were put in reservation; and in Africa there is the apartheid policy against the Blacks in Rhodesia and South Africa. In this connection see Paul Ginewski: *The Two Faces of Apartheid* (Chicago: Henry Regnery Company, 1965).

46. For example, the Spaniards intermarried with the Indians.

47. This was the condition in Algeria, and still today in South Africa, and Portuguese colonies in Africa till recently when some of them are gaining independence. Power has changed hands in Rhodesia (now called Zimbabwe) and Mugabe has become the first Black president.

48. These leaders often take great risks: they face imprisonment, torture and death. Cf., Jomo Kenyatta in Kenya during the Mau Mau Uprising (see L.S.B. Leakey: *Mau Mau and the Kikuyu: Defeating the Mau Mau*); Kwame Nkrumah in Gold Coast (now Ghana). The leaders of the Algerian Revolution (War) of Independence are a case in point.

49. This is the colonial policy of the French. See William H. Lewis, ed.: *French-Speaking Africa: The Search for Identity* (New York: Walker and Company, 1965); David C. Gordon: *North Africa's French Legacy 1954-1962,* Harvard Middle Eastern Monograph, and Cambridge: Distributed for the Center for Middle Eastern Studies of Harvard University by Harvard University

Press, 1962.

50. See Edgar O'Balance: *Op. Cit.*, p. 21.

51. See *Ibid.*, p. 21.

52. Quoted from Roger Murray and Tom Weingraf in "'The Algerian Revolution," *New Left Review*, No. 22 (London), December 1963, p. 23.

53. See Edgar O'Balance: *Op. Cit.*, p. 22.

54. *Ibid.*, pp. 28ff.

55. Etoile Norde Africaine (African North Star).

56. See Edgar O'Balance, *Op. Cit.*, p. 30.

57. See Germain Tillion: *France and Algeria, Complementary Enemies* (New York: Alfred A. Knopf, 1961), p. 135.

58. See Edgar O'Balance: *Op. Cit.*, p. 33.

59. *Ibid.*, p. 35.

60. Irene L. Gendzier: *Frantz Fanon, A Critical Study*, p. 126.

61. Fanon: *Toward the African Revolution*, pp. 47-51.

62. A *caid* is an indigenous magistrate.

63. A *fellah* is a peasant.

64. Fanon: *Toward the African Revolution*, p. 51.

65. *Ibid.*, pp. 52-54.

Chapter IV

1. Albert William Levi: *Humanism and Politics* (Bloomington, Indiana: University Press, 1969), p. 448.

2. St. Thomas Aquinas: *Summa Theologiae*, Pt. 11-11, Q. 64, Art. 3, trans. by Fathers of the English Dominican Province, Vol. Two (New York/Boston/Cincinnati/Chicago/San Francisco, 1947), p. 1467.

3. Germain G. Grisez: "Toward a Consistent Natural Law Ethics of Killing," *The American Journal of Jurisprudence*, Vol. 15 (1970), p. 69.

4. See Alan Donagan: *The Theory of Morality* (Chicago: University of Chicago Press, 1977), p. 163.

5. See Elizabeth Anscombs: "War and Murder," *War and Morality*, pp. 43-53 for a good discussion of this view.

6. See John C. Ford, S.J.: "The Morality of Obliteration Bombing," *War and Morality*, pp. 15 ff. for a good discussion of this problem.

7. See St. Thomas Aquinas: *Op. Cit.*, 11-11, Q. 64 Art. 7 Response. For a good account of the historical development of the principle of the double effect see J. Ghoos: "L'Acte a Double Effet: Etude de Theologie Positive," *Ephemerides Theologiae Lovanieusis*, XXVII (1951), pp. 30-52. Quoted from Grisez: *Op. Cit.*, p. 78.

8. See Germain Grisez: *Op. Cit.*, p. 78.

9. See Elizabeth Anscomb: "War and Murder," *War and Morality*, p. 51.

10. Peter Knauer, S.J.: "The Hermeneutic Function of the Principle of Double Effect," *Natural Law Forum*, 12 (1967), p. 137.

11. *Ibid.*, p. 133.

12. *Ibid.*, pp. 140-141.

13. *Ibid.*, p. 162.

14. *Ibid.,* p. 162.

15. Van der Marck: *Love and Fertility: Contemporary Questions about Birth Regulation* (London, Melbourne, New York: Sheed and Ward), p. 52.

16. *Ibid.,* p. 53.

17. *Ibid.,* p. 55.

18. *Ibid.,* p. 59.

19. *Ibid.,* p. 61.

20. *Op. Cit.,* p. 86.

21. *Ibid.,* p. 86.

22. *Ibid.,* p. 88.

23. *Ibid.,* p. 90.

24. *Ibid.,* p. 90.

25. *Ibid.,* p. 92.

26. See Jay Mallin: *Terror and Urban Guerillas* (Coral Gables: University of Miami Press, 1971), pp. 3ff.

27. See *Ibid.*

28. The Christian teaching of nonviolence is in place here because Christ requires a more perfect state of morality of his followers. It is based on Christian love *(caritas).* If violence, as neutrally defined as force that injures, were intrinsically evil, God would not have placed a ban on some enemies in the Old Testament. As the Creator, God is Lord of life and death; and evil is what goes against his command.

Chapter V

1. Fanon: *Toward the African Revolution,* p. 84.

2. *Ibid.,* p. 84.

3. Fanon: *The Wretched of the Earth,* p. 36.

4. See Fanon: *Toward the African Revolution,* p. 110.

5. Fanon: *The Wretched of the Earth,* p. 37.

6. Edgar O'Balance: *The Algerian Insurrection,* p. 39.

7. The CRUA became later FLN, and its army was called ALN (Armee de Liberation Nationale, Army of National Liberation).

8. This name was used by the French authorities as propaganda to discredit the revolution movement in Algeria by making it look like a band of barbarians. Fanon rejects this view.

9. See Alf Andrew Heggoy: *Insurgency and Counter-insurgency in Algeria,* p. 73.

10. See *Ibid.,* p. 182.

11. See *Ibid.,* p. 232. See Germaine Tillion: *France and Algeria,* p. 146. Tillion's estimate was between 37 and 53 dead, and 280 homeless. Quoted from Heggoy, *Op. Cit.,* p. 314.

12. See Fanon: *Toward the African Revolution,* pp. 64ff.

13. For the description of the torture see Geoffrey Bocca: *The Secret Army,* pp. 38-39. Some details of the work of the Forces of Order are contained in this book.

14. Fanon: *Toward the African Revolution,* p. 90.

15. See Fanon: *The Wretched of the Earth,* p. 41.
16. Fanon: *Black Skin, White Masks,* p. 231.
17. Fanon: *Toward the African Revolution,* p. 95.
18. Fanon: *A Dying Colonialism,* trans. by Haakon Chevalier (New York: Grove Press Inc., 1965), p. 55.
19. *Ibid.,* p. 24.
20. *Ibid.,* p. 57.
21. *Ibid.,* p. 25.
22. *"Fidal"* is somebody like a member of suicidal squad in the Islamic tradition.
23. See Fanon: *A Dying Colonialism,* p. 55.
24. Fanon: *The Wretched of the Earth,* p. 139.
25. See Fanon: *Toward the African Revolution,* p. 65; p. 101; *The Wretched of the Earth,* pp. 35ff.
26. Fanon: *Toward the African Revolution,* p. 81.
27. *Ibid.,* p. 70.
28. *Ibid.,* p. 85.
29. *Ibid.,* p. 110.
30. See *Ibid.,* p. 111.
31. Fanon: *The Wretched of the Earth,* p. 35.
32. See *Ibid.,* pp. 36 ff.
33. Fanon: *A Dying Colonialism,* p. 168.
34. Fanon: *Toward the African Revolution,* p. 172.
35. See Jan Naeveson: "Pacifism: A Philosophical Analysis," *War and Morality,* ed. by Richard Wasserstrom, pp. 63-77, for a discussion of the inconsistency and ineffectiveness of Pacifism. See also Fanon: *Toward the African Revolution,* p. 155.
36. Fanon: *The Wretched of the Earth,* p. 86.
37. *Ibid.,* p. 93.
38. *Ibid.,* p. 94.
39. *Ibid.,* p. 89.
40. *Ibid.,* p. 93.
41. *Ibid.,* p. 73.
42. Fanon: *Toward the African Revolution,* p. 144.
43. See *Ibid.,* pp. 125-126.

Chapter VI

1. Karl Jaspers: *Psychopathologie General,* French translation by Kastler and Mendousse, p. 49.
2. David Cante: *Frantz Fanon,* pp. 10-11.
3. See Colin Legum: "Pan-Africanism," New York: Frederick A. Praeger, 1962; and S. Okechukwu Mezu, ed.: *The Philosophy of Pan-Africanism,* Washington, D.C.: Georgetown University Press, 1965.
4. Five Pan-African Congresses were organized by Dr. Du Bois from 1919 to 1945. See Julius Lester, ed.: *The Thought and Writings of W.E.B. DuBois,* New York: Vintage Books, 1971, Vol. II, pp. 190-209.

5. Peter Geisman: *Op. Cit.*, p. 159.

6. Fanon: *Toward the African Revolution*, p. 177.

7. *Ibid.*, p. 179.

8. See N.D. Ukachi Onyewu: "A Relevent Utopia," *The Philosophy of Pan-Africanism.*

9. See Jewell R. Marzique: "The Emergence of African Personality," pp. 33-37; Victor C. Ferkiss: *The Philosophy of Pan-Africanism*, pp. 33-37; Victor C. Ferkiss: *Africa's Search for Identity;* Alez Quaison Sackey, *Africa Unbound,* pp. 35-58.

10. See Geismar: *Op. Cit.*, p. 146.

11. For a detailed account see, Fanon: *Toward the African Revolution*, pp. 183 ff.

12. See Fanon: *The Wretched of the Earth*, p. 105.

13. See *Ibid.*, pp. 102-106.

14. Fanon: *Toward the African Revolution*, p. 145.

15. Fanon: *The Wretched of the Earth*, p. 105. Also see the encyclical letters: Pope Paul VI, *On the Development of Peoples*, (March 20, 1967); and Pope John XXIII, *Peace on Earth* on the same theme of reconciling the human family and aid to developing nations.

16. *Ibid.*, p. 315.

Chapter VII

1. Karl Marx: "'Theses on Feuerbach," *Basic Writings* edited by Lewis S. Feuer, New York: Doubleday and Company, Inc., p. 245.

2. See Peter Geisman: *Fanon: A Biography*, p. 197.

3. Jean Paul Sartre: *Existentialism and Human Emotions*, p. 15.

4. *The Communist Manifesto*, p. 12.

5. See *Ibid.*, p. 12 ff.

6. See *Ibid.*, p. 20.

7. Emmanuel Hansen: *Frantz Fanon: Social and Political Thought*, p. 133.

8. Fanon: *The Wretched of the Earth*, p. 175.

9. *Ibid.*, p. 150.

10. *Ibid.*, p. 150.

11. *Ibid.*, p. 109.

12. See Emmanuel Hansen: *Op. Cit.*, p. 133.

13. Fanon: *The Wretched of the Earth*, pp. 111-112.

14. Fanon: *The Wretched of the Earth.*

15. *Ibid.*, p. 130.

16. *Ibid.*, p. 130.

17. See *Ibid.*, p. 137. This happened in Algeria where the lumpen-proletariat enlisted in the French army; in Angola they led the Portuguese soldiers; and in the Congo (now Zaire) they were exploited by the enemy to organize "spontaneous mass meetings against Lumumba."

18. Fanon is not alone in doing this. Michael Bakanin and Mao, Rene Dumont all share in this tradition of making the peasantry the revolutionary force.

19. *Op. Cit.*, pp. 150-151.

20. See Nguyen Nghe: "Frantz Fanon et les probleme de l-independence."
21. See David and Marina Ottaway: *Algeria: The Politics of a Socialist Revolution* (Berkeley and Los Angeles: University of California Press, 1970), p. 41.
22. Fanon: *The Wretched of the Earth,* p. 197.
23. Most newly independent African countries are now under military rule. This is not real independence.

Chapter VIII

1. See Simone de Beauvoir: *La Force des choses* (Paris: Gallimand, 1963), p. 622.
2. Fanon: *The Wretched of the Earth,* p. 109.
3. *Ibid.,* pp. 112-113.
4. For example, kings, chiefs and commoners, castes such as *osu* and *diala* in Igboland, Nigeria.
5. See Fanon: *The Wretched of the Earth,* p. 124.
6. *Ibid.,* p. 124.
7. *Ibid.,* p. 125.
8. *Ibid.,* p. 165.
9. *Ibid.,* p. 177.
10. *Ibid.,* p. 180.
11. *Ibid.,* p. 185.
12. *Ibid.,* p. 202.
13. *Ibid.,* p. 99.
14. *Ibid.,* p. 197-205.
15. *Ibid.,* p. 170.

Chapter IX

1. Aime Cesaire: "Homage to Frantz Fanon," *Presence Africaine,* Vol. 12, No. 40 (1962), p. 131.
2. Peter Geisman: *Fanon: A Biography,* p. 152.
3. *Ibid.,* p. 152.
4. Eldridge Cleaver: "An Open Letter to Stokely Carmichael," *Ramparts* (September, 1969), p. 31.
5. The civil rights movement in the United States is now divided into violent and nonviolent advocates. The latter think that Black liberation can be effected within the system using the present momentum.
6. See my article, "Frantz Fanon: A Sign of Reconciliation or Contradiction," *Philosophical Forum,* Fall/Winter, 1978/79.
7. *Op. Cit.,* p. 316.
8. Roger Garaudy: *Marxism in the Twentieth Century,* p. 36.
9. See Conald Clark Hodges: *Socialist Humanism,* pp. 337-338.
10. Fanon: *Black Skin, White Masks,* p. 232.

NAME INDEX

A

Abbas, Ferhat, 51, 52, 62, 64
Accra, v, viii, 98, 116, 117
Addis Ababa, 98, 117
Adler, Alfred, iii, vii, 35, 45, 55
Africa, i, ii, v, viii, xiii, 2, 32, 40, 41, 46
  56, 74, 88, 89, 95, 96, 98, 107, 114,
  115, 117
Afro-Asian Solidarity Conference in Con-
  akry, Guinea, 98, 117
Alcidamas, 15, 21
Alexis, Jaques, v, viii
Algerian, Algeria, i, iv, v, vi, vii, ix, 49, 50,
  52, 53, 56, 59, 61, 63, 65, 69, 80, 81,
  82, 83, 86, 89, 96, 97, 99, 100, 102,
  103, 106, 107, 121, 127
Algerian Provisional Government, v, viii
Algiers, iv, vii, 12, 16, 34, 49, 60, 82, 83,.
  98, 99
All-African Peoples' Conference, v, viii
ALN, 81, 98
America, 46, 56
Andre, 43, 53
Angola, 98, 117
Antilles, i, ii, v, 44, 54
Antiphon, 14, 20, 21
Aristotle, 4, 6, 7, 14, 20, 26, 34, 110, 130
Asia, 74, 88
Aures Mountain, 81, 97

B

Benin, 95, 114
Biafra, 95, 114
Black Skin, White Masks (Peau Noir,
  Masques Blancs), iii, vii, 2, 4
Blida-Joinville, iv, vii, 56, 68
Bordeaux, 44, 54

Boupacha, Djamila, 83, 99
Bugeand, 49, 60

C

Calvert, Peter, 3, 6
Cameroons, 98, 117
Capecia, Mayotte, 43, 53
Carmichael, Stokely, 102, 114, 121, 134
Casbah, 82, 99
Caute, David, 96, 115
Ce'saire, Aimé, iii, v, vii, viii, 44, 54, 113,
  134
Chalmers, Johnson, 5, 7
Charles X, 49, 60
Chauffie, Martin, M., 89, 106
Cicero, 1, 3
Cleaver, Eldridge, 114, 134
Congo, 98, 117
Congress of Black Writers and Artists, v, viii
Coser, Lewis, xii, xiii, 1, 2
Creole, 43, 52
Czech, 27, 35

D

Deming, Barbara, 9, 12
Diagne, Blaise, M., 97, 116
Dien Bien Phu, 81, 97
Diop, Alioune, v, viii
Donagan, Alan, 62, 75
Dublé, Josie, iv, vii
Du Bois, Burghardt, W.E., 97, 116

E

Eckstein, Harry, 5, 7
Ellwood, Charles, 5, 7
El Moudjahid, v, viii

ENA, 51, 52, 62, 63
England, 47, 57
Ethiopia, 95, 114
Europe, ii, vi, 29, 37, 47, 56, 57, 74, 88, 99, 102, 115, 117, 118, 121, 136

F

Fanon, Felix, iii, vi
Fanon, Frantz, i, ii, iii, iv, v, vi, vii, viii, xii, 1
Fanon, Joby, ii, vi
Feuerbach, 39, 50
F.L.N. (Front de Liberatione Nationale), v, viii, 74, 81, 83, 88, 98, 99, 100
Forte-de-France, i, v
France, i, v, 50, 52, 61, 63, 81, 89, 97, 107
Franco-African Unity, 98, 117
French Communist Party, 52, 63
Freud, iii, vii, 35, 45

G

Geisman, Peter, 101, 114, 120, 134
Gendzier, Irene L., 12, 16, 53, 64
General de Gaulle, 52, 63
General de Lattre de Tassigny, ii, vi
General Girand, 52, 63
Germans, ii, vi
Ghana, v, viii, 95, 98, 114, 116, 117
God, 1, 3, 30, 50
Gorgias, 15, 21
Grisez, Germain G., 62, 67, 69, 75, 81, 82, 82A, 83, 84, 85
Guinea, 98, 117

H

Hadj, Messoli, 51, 52, 62, 63
Hansen, Emmanuel, 103, 106, 122, 125
Hegel, iii, vii, 16, 22, 23, 28, 30, 35, 36, 37 39, 45, 46, 47, 48, 49, 90, 102, 108, 121
Heidegger, iii, vii
Hyksos ('Shepherd Kings'), 4, 6

I

India, 46, 56
Indochina, 81, 97
Irish Republican Army (IRA), 74, 88

J

Jacobinism, xii, 1
Jaspers, iii, vii, 45, 55
Jews, 19, 26, 44, 54
Jung, iii, vii

K

Kameka, Eugene, 5, 7
Kant, Immanuel, 16, 22
Kennedy, John F., 90, 107
Kenya, 98, 117
Kierkegaard, iii, vii
Knauer, Peter, 67, 81, 82

L

Lacoste, Robert, 82, 98
Lamont, Corliss, 1, 3
L'an V de la Revolution Algerienne (A Dying Colonialism), v, viii
Latin America, 74, 88
Lenin, iii, vii
Les Damnes de la Terre (The Wretched of the Earth), v, viii
Levi, Albert W., 58, 71
Locke, John, 6, 8
Lumumba, Patrice, 98, 117
Lyon, iv, vii

M

Malagasy, 42, 52
Mali, 98, 117
Mannoni, M., 42, 52
Martinique, i, iii, v, vii, 43, 53
Marx, Karl, iii, vii, 4, 7, 25, 29, 30, 31, 33, 35, 36, 38, 39, 40, 41, 45, 46, 49, 51, 52, 56, 94, 101, 103, 107, 113, 120, 122, 126
Miller, Ronald B., 7, 10
Morocco, 50, 61
Moumie, Felix, 98, 117

N

Napoleon, 49, 60
National Institutes of Health, Bethesda,

Maryland, U.S.A., vi, viii
National Liberation Front of Algeria (FLN), v, viii, 74, 81, 83, 88, 98, 99, 100
Nazis, 19, 26
Negro, 18, 21, 25, 26, 29, 33, 41, 43, 44, 46, 52, 53, 54, 56, 96, 115
NFL, 86, 103
Nietzsche, iii, vii, 2, 4
Nisbet, Robert, xii, 1
Nkrumah, Kwame, 98, 117

O

O'Balance, Edgar, 49, 60

P

Palestinian Liberation Organization (PLO), 74, 88
Pan-African Congress, first, 97, 116
Paris, v, viii, 43, 53
Peau Noir, Masques Blancs (Black Skin, White Masks), iii, vii, 2, 4
Plato, 23, 30, 31, 39, 58, 71
Polybius, 4, 7
Ponty, Merleau, iii, vii
Popular Front Government, 52, 63
Pour la Revolution Africaine (Toward the African Revolution), vi, ix
PPA, 52, 63

Q

R

Roberto, Holden, 98, 117
Rome, v, 7, 98, 117
Rousseau, Jean Jacques, 25, 32, 33

S

Saint Alban, iii, vii
Saint Arnand, 49, 60
Saint Thomas Aquinas, 61, 66, 75, 80
Sakiet Sidi Youssef, 83, 99
Sartre, J.P., iii, v, vii, viii, 35, 45, 101, 102, 120, 121

Schacht, 39, 49
Second Conference of African Peoples in Tunis, 98, 117
Second Congress of Black Writers in Rome, 98, 117
Senghor, Leopold, v, viii
Setif, 53, 54, 64, 65
Siegel, J.E., xii, 1
Simone de Beauvoir, i, v, viii
Smith, Ian, 113, 134
Socrates, 13, 19, 25, 33, 58, 71, 115, 136
Soummam, 82, 98
Soustelle, Jacques, 81, 97

T

Tam-Tam, iii, vi
Third Conference of Independent African States at Addis-Ababa, 98, 117
Thrasymachus, 25, 33
Tosquelles, Francois, iii, vii
Trotsky, iii, vii
Tunisia, 50, 61

U

Ulema, 51, 62
Union of Students from Overseas France, iii, vi
United Nations, 99, 118
United States, 20, 27, 113, 134
University of Lyons, France, iii, vi
U.S.S.R., vi, viii

V

Van der Marck, W., 67, 68, 81, 82, 82A
Vauclin, iii, vii
Veneuse, Jean, 44, 54
Vichy Government, 52, 63
Viet Cong, 74, 88
Vlastos, Gregory, 23, 31

W

Winslow, 47, 57
Wright, Richard, v, viii
Wurttenberg, 38, 48

X

Y

Z

Zaire, 98, 117

SUBJECT INDEX

A

Africa and the world, 95-100, 114-119
African unity, v, viii, 97, 99, 115, 118
Algerian war,
    revolution, 96-113
Alienation, 2, 3, 5
    definition of, 35, 45
    in Fanon, 41-45, 51-55
    in Hegel, 36-39, 46-50
    in Karl Marx, 39-40, 50-51
    of the colonized, 44, 45, 51-55
    of the Negroes, 41-45, 51-55
Army, 111, 131

B

Battle of Algiers, 82, 98
Black, i, ii, iii, v, vi, vii, xii, 1, 15, 21, 22, 25
    29, 30, 33, 36, 38, 43, 45, 53, 55, 115, 136
    problem, 15, 22
Blume-Viollette Bill, 51, 62
Bourgeoisie, 103-104, 122-123

C

Case of Algeria, 49-57, 59-69
Coercion, 10, 13
Collective unconscious, 44, 54
Colonial,
    imperialism,
        ethics of, 46-49, 56-59
    revolution, 6, 8
    system, iii, iv, vii, 45-57, 55-69
Colonialism, 25, 27, 32, 33, 35, 41, 45, 55
    88, 89, 106-107
Colour,
    prejudice, ii, vi, 43, 53
Consciousness, 2, 4

Consistency or contradiction,
    problem of, xii, 1, 79-94, 95-113
Crisis,
    of humanism, 15, 21
Criticism,
    of Fanon for not conducting revolution
    in Martinique, i-ii, v-vi
Cultural revolution, 109, 129
Culture,
    dialects of racism and culture, 32-33,
    41-43

D

Decentralization, 110, 130
Decolonization, 6, 8, 11, 12, 15, 16, 31-34
    40-43
Dehumanization,
    acts of, ii, v, 19, 26
Democracy, 4, 6
Dialectic, 2, 3
    Hegel's concept of, 30, 39
    of Master and Slave, 22
Dialectical character, 30, 38, 135
Double Effect,
    principle of, 66, 80

E

Education, 1, 3
    in the colonial world, 48, 59
Epitaph,
    Fanon's, vi, ix
European humanism, 2, 3

F

Frantz Fanon,
    family origin, ii, v

humanism, xiii, 2
Force, 10, 13
Freedom, 1, 2, 3, 4, 5, 8, 21, 28
    anguish of, 12, 16, 18, 25

G

H

Human dignity or recognition, 13-20, 19-28
    Hegel's concept, 16, 22
Humaness in the world of the mentally ill,
    introduction of, iv, vii
Humanism, xii, xiii, 1, 2, 3, 4, 5
Human rights, 3, 5

I

Innocent,
    defining the, 64, 77-78
    killing the innocent, 2, 64-66, 78-80

J

Justice, 2, 3, 4, 5, 22-26, 30-35

K

L

Leukemia,
    Fanon sick of, v-vi, viii-ix
Love, 2, 3, 4, 5, 26-27, 34-35
Lumpen-proletariat, 105-107, 124-126

M

Manichean world, 45-46, 55-56
Manicheism, 93, 111

N

Nationalist parties, 108-110, 128-129
Negro Slave, 18, 25
New humanism,
    project of, xii, 1, 2, 3, 4, 5, 13, 19, 25
New man,
    emergence of, 29-30, 37-38

Non-violence, xiii, 2, 108, 113, 115, 116,
    128, 134, 136-137

O

P

Pan-Africanism, 97, 115-116
Peace, 3, 5, 26-27, 34-35
Political,
    education,
        (conscientization) of the masses, 107,
        126
    revolution, 3, 4, 5, 6
Praxis,
    revolutionary, 101-107, 120-127
Pressure, 10, 14
Principle of Self-defense, xii, xiii, 1, 2
Proletariat, 103-104, 122-123

Q

R

Rebellion, 3, 6
    relation of rebellion to revolution, 3, 5
Reconciliation of humanism and violence,
    problem of, 72, 79, 86, 95
Renaissance, 1, 3
Reparation for Colonial injustice, 99-100,
    118-119
Revolution, i, ii, v, xii, xiii, 1, 2, 3-5, 5-8,
    38, 48
    and violence,
        relation of, 4-5, 7-8
    Fanon's concept of, 5-6, 8-9
Revolutionary,
    agencies, 102, 121
    humanism, i, iv, v, vii, xii, xiii, 1, 2, 33,
        43, 102, 108, 110, 121, 128, 130

S

Self-defense, 60-64, 73-77
Slavery, 15, 21, 29
Social revolution, 3, 5
Socialism, 110, 130
Socio-political ideal, xiii, 2, 108-112,
    128-133

SUBJECT INDEX

T

Terror,
  terrorism, xiii, 2, 4, 6, 74-78, 88-92
Torture, 2, 72-74, 86-88

U

Universal,
  humanism, iii, vi
  man, 1, 3
Universalist,
  character, 27-29, 35-37
  humanism, xii, 1, 3, 5

V

Violence, iv, viii, xiii, 2, 4, 7
  and genuine humanism,
    problem of, xii, 1
  and revolution,

relation of, 4-5, 7-8
definition of, 6, 9
Fanon's concept of, 8, 11, 12, 14
justifying, 58-78, 71-94
remarks on, 59-60, 72-73
the effects of, 10-12, 14-15

W

White, i, ii, iii, v, vi, vii, 15, 21, 22, 25, 28,
  29, 30, 33, 36, 38, 43, 44, 53, 54, 55
  115, 136
Women,
  place of, 111, 131

X

Y

Z